JERUSALEM

On Religious Power and Judaism

PREFACE 5

SECTION I. 12

SECTION II. 66

TRANSLATOR'S NOTES 149

PREFACE

Every nation has its own disposition and exigences, its own notions and aptitudes; they have their root in its first origin, their substantiality and continuance in its mode of organization; and as essential properties, they are, therefore, inseparable from its existence. An unbiassed observer of mankind will not look for those properties in things secondary and incidental, nor is it in the general human character that he will frivolously strive to discover the cause of their being; for there he will find only *Man*, — and not the *Accidental*, the *National*, which distinguishes one set of men from another.

There is not, therefore, any nation which can be pronounced utterly incapable of cultivation, or of improvement and refinement in manners. If it can be proved that the elements of its character were originally good, and that its matter and form suited with its intrinsic worth; no one will dispute, but that it could only be the particular circumstances in the long vicissitudinous course of its history, which, having by little and little put the Jewish nation out of its right point of view, have remodeled the whole, and made it appear in an altered, and, not unfrequently, a disadvantageous shape. Remove those disadvantages, and the Jewish polity will at once assume an attitude of dignity and respect. Only the training must go forth from the nation itself; and the germ of self-cultivation must expand itself anew, else all our endeavours will be fruitless. Salutary effects may only then be reasonably expected, when innate though dormant powers are stimulated afresh; then shall we have the pleasure of beholding in the great garden of God, the flower, once ready to sink down, bloom again, raise her drooping head, and go on flourishing by the side of — and in the best harmony with — her sparkling sisters: whereas foreign cultivation, or that introduced from without, whether forced on or borrowed, would either annihilate her altogether, or at least suppress and deform her. Neither individual man nor entire nations will admit of being re-fashioned after foreign patterns. Organizing Nature has assigned to every kind of matter, as well as to every climate, its particular capabilities and productions; and Art can effect nothing except it fall back upon the indigenous soil.

Hence the great men of all nations, once seized with the ardour of perfectioning their contemporaries, have founded their intended improvements on maxims already extant. Acquainted with the human heart, they considered it a paramount duty to be as tender as possible, with that which was held most sacred by the people they had to deal with. The old was merely made to assume a more modern form, and, by a new and better appearance, which they well knew how to give it, adapted to their noble design, in conformity to times and local situations. They did not despotically deviate from whatsoever was generally recognized, and generally venerated; it was not everything that they condemned and arbitrarily declared unfit; that only which was really harmful, which outraged God and man, they vigorously sought to put down. Detrimental abuses hallowed by superstition, erroneous opinions leading astray, immoral proceedings varnished over by zealots with the colour of religion, were marked as infirmities in social man, and removed on account of their noxiousness. It was thus that those Philosophers succeeded in becoming useful to the age they lived in, knowing, like a certain Rabbi,[1] wisely to separate the bitter husk from the savory kernel. And if the excellent axioms which they strove to diffuse were not received with equal alacrity everywhere, yet time has vindicated the tendency of their undertaking, upon the whole; while posterity is ejaculating thanks and blessings on the memory of those guardian angels of humanity.[2]

There was a time when the Hebrew people, faithful to the bliss-fraught religion of their forefathers, could count themselves among the happiest nations on earth. Manners and customs then qualified them as a people consecrated to God, who by their moral and political constitution most gloriously distinguished themselves from any other Nation then existing. At that happy period it was, that, favoured by temporary circumstances, the Israelite people attained a certain high degree of perfection, nationality exalting itself to general philanthropy, while, under the auspices of a pacific Monarchy the salutary effect of peace to the nation failed not to manifest itself. With that wisdom which the pious idea of an eternal and universal Father alone could support, they widened the horizon, and enlarged their sympathies for those of a different opinion;[3] and toleration, content, peace and happiness, pervaded the mind of the nation. And whence did they derive that pious spirit? From Religion; from her who, throughout, lays the greatest stress on brotherly love and the moral worth of man; from her, with whom reason and eternal truth, virtue and justice, are the main rule and constant aim.

But not only to the flourishing house of Jacob, did Religion offer tenets and laws conducive to salvation; in her there are, besides, peculiar comforting and encouraging promises to the dispersed flock of Israel. When the national independence ceased, and the emigrant members of the nation wandered about all parts of the world, they took away with them, of all their treasures, nothing but their religion. She wandered with them in all directions; with her, those poor victims of tyranny sought and found aid and consolation. Despite of all scoffing and contumely, despite of the many persecutions they had to endure for her sake, they continued true to her, the more true, the greater the cruelties exercised toward them.

After overcoming many sufferings, after various revolting and barbarous treatment, which rendered mankind more and more hateful to those tormented men, they returned into the bosom of the *Divine One*, there to gather fresh strength, fresh resolution, firmly to encounter still more cruel destinies lowering with crushing weight over their heads. — But wherefore these gloomy pictures of former ages? The noble-minded turn away disgustingly from these appalling scenes, to where more agreeable objects tempt his view. Then let me throw a veil over this horrid part, and skip that page in the records of our hapless ancestors, lest I should again depress our spirits now raised by modern and better scenes to the most pleasing expectation. A new chapter commences in the history of the Jews opening with gladder events, and becoming more and more cheerful and pleasant as it proceeds. The minds of most nations are now regulated by *the rules of Equity*; the iron barrier which separated the hearts of men for thousands of years past, the spirit of toleration has pulled down. *Humanity* is the watchword sounding from every tongue, and approximating to each other the hearts of all men. On the Jewish nation, too, this change is exerting a very salutary influence. Men begin to think of, and feel sympathy for, the Jew, too, being well aware of the wrong done him in former ages, by debarring him from his just share of the common stock of humanity; well aware of the *aggravated* wrong done him, in ousting him, at the same time, of the means whereby he might participate of that common stock. Thank God! the times are over, when the ideas of *Jew and Man* were considered heterogeneous. The Jew, too, now feels his worth as a man; and he feels it with thanks to his fellowmen. His inner consciousness tells him, that he too is destined by nature to apply his faculties for the welfare of the whole.

But all the obstacles are not removed yet. The wild bee of raw uncultivated ages has left a dangerous sting behind in innermost mankind, which cannot be extracted but with the wisest caution. On the one part, they think they have discovered in the Jews' system of conduct, nothing but immoral motives, and absolutely set them down as an isolated set of men. On the other hand, much remains yet to be done; many a notion wants refining: much of what is defective requires to be supplied; and a world of misapprehension to be explained and set to rights.

To elucidate the foregoing assertions by historical and literary data, is in a great measure the object of the present undertaking, which, as far as the "Jerusalem" is concerned, I had been advised twelve years ago to consign to the press, by several individuals who honored my "Memoirs of Moses Mendelssohn" with their approbation. Now the want of leisure, which then prevented me from following their suggestion has, alas! changed into too great an abundance, and I have deemed it expedient in presenting a translation of "Jerusalem" to the British Public, to accompany the same with those publications which were the cause of that extraordinary production, some of which have become very scarce; and to add thereto, in the form of notes, a selection of the most approved articles' by several Jewish authors, all more or less connected with, or bearing on the main subject. Perhaps it may be as well here to observe to the generality of my readers of either religious persuasion, that, in the character of a Disciple, as I fairly may be supposed to be, of the leading system of this work, I do not (with the exception of a very few interspersed remarks of my own), by any means hold myself accountable for every thesis, doctrine, or opinion, broached or laid down in the same. Too obscure for a censor, too timid for a reformer, and too conscious of my own defects for a satirist, my ambition, in this instance, soars no higher than the hope of having furnished a tolerable translation; and even in this I may be disappointed, unless, on being arraigned for inaccuracy of style, an indulgent Public would, in extenuation, admit my plea: that I am not — what, without any disparagement of my own country, I should esteem an honour — a native of this.

Moses Samuel

SECTION I.

To oppose those props of social life, state and church, civil and ecclesiastical government, secular and spiritual power to each other, so that they shall counterpoise, and not, on the contrary, prove burdens on social life; nor press on its foundation, in a greater degree than they help to support its structure, is in politics one of the most difficult problems, with the solution of which they are occupied already since many ages, and have here and there, perhaps with greater success, practically compromised, than theoretically solved it. These different relations of man in a state of society, it was thought proper to separate as moral entities, and to assign to each a separate jurisdiction, separate rights, dues, power and domain; although neither the precincts of those jurisdictions, nor the lines which divide them have yet been accurately fixed. Now the church is seen to move the landmark far up the territory of the state; and then the state to presume encroachments, which according to accepted notions, seem no less usurping. The evils which have hitherto arisen from a disagreement between those moral entities, and still threaten to arise, are immense. When in the field against each other, mankind is the victim of their discord; and when they agree together, the brightest jewel of human happiness is gone; for they seldom agree but for the purpose of banishing from their realms, *a third moral entity*, liberty of conscience, which knows how to derive some advantage from their squabbles.

Despotism has one advantage, it is cogent. However troublesome its demands may be found by common sense, they are themselves systematical and well-connected. It has a definite answer to every question. Never mind limits; for with him who has got all, "more or less" is of no farther consideration. So is, according to Roman Catholic principles, also ecclesiastical government; it is complete in every particular, and as it were all of one piece. Grant it all its demands; and you will at least know what you have to expect. Your system is built for you, and perfect repose reigns in every part of it; it is true, that kind of dismal repose which, as Montesquieu says, "reigns in a fortress on the eve of its being stormed." Yet he by whom a quiet doctrine and a quiet life are considered happiness, will find that happiness no where better secured to him, than under a Roman Catholic despot; and as even under him power is too much divided, no where better than under the absolute sway of the church herself.

But when liberty ventures to displace anything in that systematical building, dilapidation instantly threatens on all sides; and at length, it is difficult to say how much of it will keep upright. Hence the extraordinary distraction, the civil as well as ecclesiastical disturbances, at the time of the Reformation, and the obvious perplexity of the preachers and reformers themselves, whenever they had to fix the extent of rights and privileges. It was not only practically difficult, to keep within bounds the multitude let loose from their trammels, but even as to theory, we find the writings of those times full of vague and wavering ideas; whenever the ascertaining the limits of ecclesiastical power is of the question. The despotism of the Roman church was abolished; but what other form was to be substituted for it? Even now, in our enlightened times, the textbooks of canon law, could not be freed of that undeterminatedness. The clergy will not or cannot give up their claim to a regular constitution, and yet no one rightly knows in what it is to consist. Doctrinal differences are to be adjusted, yet no supreme judge is recognised; an independent church is still referred to, yet no one knows where it is to be found; claims to authority and rights are proffered, yet no one can show who is to exercise and uphold them!

Thomas Hobbes lived at a period, when fanaticism blended with inordinate love of liberty, no longer knew any bounds, and was about (as at last it did,) to bring royal authority under its foot, and entirely subvert the constitution of the realm. Disgusted with civil broils, and by nature fond of a tranquil and contemplative life, he looked on peace and safety as the greatest of blessings, no matter how procured; and those desiderata he thought were to be found only in the unity and indivisibility of the highest authority in the state. Accordingly he judges most advisable for the public good, that every thing, even men's opinions of right and wrong, should be under the superintendence of the civil authorities. And in order to do so with the greater convenience, he assumed that man has, naturally, a right to all nature endowed him with the faculty of; that a state of nature is a state of general confusion and uproar, *a war of all against all*, in which every one may do whatever he can do, and in which might constitutes right. That deplorable state lasted until mankind agreed upon putting a term to their misery, by foregoing as far as public safety was concerned, right and might, and place both in the hands of a chief magistrate elected by themselves; and henceforward whatever that magistrate ordered, was right.

Hobbes either had no taste for civil freedom, or wished it to be quashed altogether, rather than have it thus abused. But that he might reserve to himself freedom of thinking, of which he made more practice than any one else, he had recourse to a sly turn. According to his system, all right is grounded on power, and all engagement on fear. Now God being infinitely superior in power to the civil magistrate, God's rights, too, must be infinitively above the magistrate's, and the fear of God engage us to duties which are not to yield to fear of the magistrate. This, however, must be understood of internal religion, in which alone the philosopher was interested: external religion he entirely subjected to the dictates of the civil magistrate; and every innovation in religious matters without his authority, is not only high treason, but even sacrilege. The collisions which must arise between internal and external religion, he seeks to remove by the most subtle distinctions; and although there yet remain behind so many openings which betray the weakness of the union, one cannot help admiring the ingenuity with which he strives to give cogency to his system.

There is, in the main, much truth in all Hobbes's positions; and the absurd conclusions to which they lead, flow merely from the extravagant mode in which he expounds them, either from a love of the paradox, or in compliance with the taste of his times. Nor were the ideas of the law of nature, in part, sufficiently clear in those days; and Hobbes deserves as highly of moral philosophy, as Spinoza does of metaphysics; his ingenious deviation occasioned inquiry. The ideas of right and duty, power and engagement, were further developed; men learned to distinguish more correctly between physical and moral power, between violence and qualification; and these distinctions they so intimately united with the language, that, at present, the refutation of Hobbes's system seems to be in the nature of common sense, and, as it were, in that of the language. This is a property of all moral truths; when they are elucidated, they instantly are so imbibed by the language of conversation, and become so united with men's daily notions, that they will be intelligible to the meanest understanding; and we wonder how we could have stumbled before on such a level ground. But we do not consider the expenditure at which that path was cut through the wilderness.

Hobbes himself must have been sensible, in more than one respect, of the inadmissible results to which his extravagant positions immediately led. If, by nature, men be bound to no duty whatsoever, then they are not even under the obligation of keeping their compacts. If, in a state of nature, there be no engagements but what are founded on fear and powerlessness, then compacts will stand good only as long as they are supported by fear and powerlessness; then have mankind, by compacts, not advanced a step nearer to security, and still find themselves in the primitive state of universal warfare. But if compacts are to stand good, man must, by nature, and without compacts or agreements, not be qualified to act against a compact entered into by him of his own free will; that is, he must no be allowed to do so, even if he could; he must not have the moral power, even if he have the physical. *Right* and Might are, therefore, two different things; and in a state of nature too, they were hetreogeneous ideas. Hobbes, furthermore, prescribes to the highest authorities in the state, strict rules not to insist on any thing which may be contrary to the subject's welfare. For although that authority have not to account for its acts and deeds to mortal man, it has to the supreme Judge of the world, who sufficiently revealed to us his will about this. Hobbes is very ample on this; and, every thing considered, less indulgent to the gods of the earth, than his system would lead one to expect. But may not that fear of the Almighty, which is to bind sovereigns and potentates to certain duties to their subjects, become, in the state of nature, a source of engagement to every individual man as well? And so there would still be a *solemn* law of nature, which Hobbes, however, will not admit of. Thus may, in our days, any tyro in the law of nature, gain a triumph over Thomas Hobbes, which he would have to thank that philosopher for, after all.

Locke, who also lived at that period of main confusion, sought to protect liberty of conscience in another manner. In his letters on education, he puts down as a basis, the definition, that the state is a society of men united for the purpose of conjointly promoting their temporal welfare. Hence it follows, that the state has no business at all to concern itself about the citizens' persuasions regarding their eternal happiness; and that it is to tolerate every one who conducts himself civilly well, that is, who offers no obstruction to the temporal happiness of his fellow-citizens. The state, in its quality of state, is not to take notice of difference of religion. For religion, of itself, has not, of necessity, an influence in temporal affairs; and its being connected with them, depends entirely on the will of man.

Very good! If the dispute admit of being decided by a mere definition of words, I do not know a more convenient one; and if, by it, his turbulent contemporaries had let themselves be talked out of their intolerance, honest Locke himself would not have had to wander so many times into exile. "But," said they, "what should prevent us from promoting our spiritual welfare as well? Indeed, what reason have we to confine the object of social life to temporal affairs only? If mankind can at all promote their future felicity by public institutions, is it not naturally their duty to do so? Are they not in reason bound to congregate and form a social union also for that purpose? Since, then, it is so; and the state, in its quality of state, will act in secular affairs only, the question arises: to whom are we to commit the care of spiritual affairs? To the church? There we are, all of a sudden, again on the very spot from which we started! State and Church; care of temporal affairs, care of spiritual affairs, civil and ecclesiastical power. The former stands in the same relation to the latter, as the importance of temporal affairs to the importance of spiritual. The state, therefore, is subordinate to the church, and must give way in cases of collision. And now resist, who can, Cardinal Bellarmin, and his redoubtable train of arguments, to prove that the head of the church, in his quality of God's vice-gerent on earth, has, on behalf of the Lord, the stewardship of every thing temporal; and, therefore, at least, indirectly,[4] a *Regale* of all goods and minds in this world; that all secular realms are under the dominion of that spiritual Potentate, and bound to follow his directions, as to changing their form of government, deposing their kings, and putting others in their stead; because very often, the eternal salvation of the state cannot be consummated in any other manner; besides many other maxims of his order, which Bellarmin lays down with so much subtilty, in his book. *De Romane Pontifice.* Of all that has been opposed to the Cardinal's sophism, in very bulky tomes, nothing appears to hit the mark, as long as the state gives the care of eternity entirely out of its hands. Considered in another light, it is, in the strictest sense neither consonant with truth, nor does it tend to the good of man, when we cut time so clean off eternity. In the main, eternity will never fall to the share of man, his eternity is merely perpetual time; his time never ends, and is, therefore, an actual and integral part of his perduration. It is confounding ideas to oppose his temporal welfare to his eternal felicity. And this confounding of ideas is not without practical consequences. It puts the sphere of human abilities out of its proper place, and strains man's powers beyond the limits set to them by Providence with such infinite wisdom. "On the dark path on which man is to walk here on earth," (if I may be allowed to quote from my own writings) "just as much light is provided, as he wants for to make the next step. More would only dazzle, and every side-light bewilder him."[5] It is essential that man should be constantly reminded, that with death there is not a complete end of him; on the contrary, an interminable futurity awaits him, to which his earthly life is only a preparation; the same as all through Nature every present is a preparation for a future. The Rabbins liken this life to a lobby, in which we are to fit ourselves in the manner we wish to appear in the inner-room. Then take heed you no longer put this life as the opposite of futurity, and lead men to think that their true welfare in this world is not all one with their eternal welfare in the next; that it is one thing to be mindful of our happiness here, another of our happiness there, and that we may continue to enjoy the former while neglecting the latter. The short-sighted man who has to walk along a narrow path, finds his station and horizon displaced by those sort of insinuations, is in danger of getting dizzy, and of stumbling on level ground. How many a one dares not venture to partake of the present bounties of Providence, for fear he should be mulcted of an equal portion in the life to come? How many a one has turned out a bad citizen on earth, in hopes of thereby becoming so much the better a one of heaven?

I sought to obtain a clear and distinct view of the ideas of church and state, of their reciprocal influence, and on the happiness of civil life, by the following contemplations. When man becomes aware that out of society, he is as unable to discharge his duty to himself, and to the author of his existence as those to his neighbour, and thus can no longer continue in that lone condition without feeling his wretchedness, he is bound to instantly leave it, and join his species in a state of society, in order to supply their common wants by 'mutual aid, and promote the public good by joint measures. But the public good embraces the future as well as the present, the spiritual as well as the temporal. Unless we discharge our duties, we must not look for happiness either now or hereafter, either on earth or in heaven. Now, to truly discharge our duties, two things are required; namely, action and persuasion. By action is performed what duty bids, while persuasion causes it to flow from the true source, that is, to be performed from pure motives.

Action and persuasion are therefore required for the perfection of man, and it behoves society to take every possible care of both by their joint endeavours, that is, by giving the actions of its members a tendency to the public good, and by occasioning persuasions which engender such actions. The one is the governing, the other the training of civilized man. It is on grounds that man is led to either; to actions, by motivating; to persuasions, by evidential grounds. Hence society is bound to regulate both so as to make them coincide for the public good.

The grounds which lead man to rational actions and persuasions, rest partly on the relations of men to each other, partly on their relations to their creator and preserver. Those pertain to the state, these to religion. So far as men's actions and persuasions may be made subservient to public utility, on grounds arising from their relations to each other, they are an object fit for the civil government; but so far as they are assumed to spring from the relations of man to God, they come under the cognizance of the church, the synagogue, or the mosque. We meet in so many textbooks of canon law as it is called, with grave enquiries: whether Jews, heretics, and misbelievers, may not respectively constitute churches? Considering the immense prerogatives, which the thing called *Church* is wont to usurp, the question is not so absurd, as it must appear to an unbiassed reader. With me, however, the difference of names, as may be supposed, is of no great consequence. All such public institutions for the cultivation of man, as refer to his relations to God, I call *Church*; and those which refer to his relations to man, I call *State*. By the cultivation of man, I mean the endeavouring to manage both action and persuasion, so as to make them jointly conduce to happiness; say, training and governing man.

Happy the state which succeeds in governing the people by education itself; I mean by instilling in their minds such morals and principles, as of themselves lead to actions of public utility, and need not be constantly impelled by the spur of the laws. Man, in a state of society, is obliged to forego many of his rights for the public good, or as it may be called, to sacrifice frequently his own interest to beneficence. Now he feels happy whenever that sacrifice is made from his own impulse, whenever he sees that it was made by him solely on behalf of beneficence. In the main, beneficence renders happier than self-interest; but we must feel ourselves by it, and the manifesting of our powers. Not, as some sophists explain it, because self-love is all with man; but because beneficence is no longer such, nor carries any value or merit with it, when it does not arise from the spontaneous impulse of the beneficent.

This will perhaps enable us to give a satisfactory answer to the famous question: "Which form of government is the best?" a question which has hitherto been replied to in so many different ways seemingly all correct alike. The fact, however, is: it is too indefinite a question, nearly as much so as another of the same sort in medicine, viz. "Which kind of food is wholesomest?" Every constitution, every climate, every age, sex, profession, &c. requires a different answer. And so does our politico-philosophical problem. For every people, for every stage of civilization at which that people has arrived, another form of government may be the best. Many despotically-ruled nations would feel very miserable were they left to govern themselves; and so would high-spirited republicans if subjected to a monarch. Nay, many a nation, as improvements, general habits and principles undergo changes in it, will change also its form of government, and in a course of ages, run the whole round from anarchy to absolutism in all their shades and modifications, and yet be found to have all along chosen the form of government, which was best for them under existing circumstances.

But under every circumstance, and with every proviso, I think it an unerring standard of a good government, the more there is under it, wrought by morality and persuasions, and accordingly, the more the people are governed by education itself. In other words, the more opportunity there is given the citizen to see evidently, that he foregoes some of his rights for the public good only; that he sacrifices part of his own interest to beneficence only; and that therefore he gains on the one side, as much by acts of beneficence, as, on the other, he loses by sacrifices. Nay, that by sacrificing, he even profits in inward happiness, because it enhances the merit and dignity of the action, and, therefore also encreases the true perfection of the beneficent himself. So it is, for instance, not advisable for the state to charge itself with all offices of philanthropy, not even the distributing of charity excepted, and convert them into public establishments. Man feels his own worth when he is acting liberally; when it is obvious to him that by his gift he alleviates the distress of a fellow-creature; that is, when he gives, because he *pleases*; but when he gives because he *must*, he feels only his fetters.

It ought therefore to be the chief endeavour of the state, to govern mankind by morals and persuasions. Now there is no other way of improving men's principles, and by means of them also their morals, but conviction. Laws will not alter persuasions; Arbitrary punishments or rewards generate no maxims, nor do they improve morals. Fear and hope are no criterions of truth. Knowledge, reasoning, convictions, they alone bring forth principles which, through credit and example, may pass into manners. And there it is where religion must step in to assist the state, and the church become the supporter of civil happiness. It behoves her to convince the people, in the most emphatic manner of the truth of noble sentiments and persuasions; to show them that the duties to man are also duties to God, the transgressing of which is itself the greatest misery; that serving one's country is true religion; probity and justice the commandment of God; charity his most holy will; and that a right knowledge of the Creator, will not let misanthropy harbor long in the creature's heart. To teach this, is the office, duty, and vocation of the church; to preach it, the office, duty and vocation of her ministers. How could it ever have entered men's thoughts to let the Church teach, and her ministers preach quite the reverse?

But when the character of a people, the stage of civilization at which it has arrived, a population swelled along with its national prosperity, multiplied relations and alliances, overgrown luxury, and other causes render it impossible to govern it by persuasions only, the state has recourse to public institutions, compulsory laws, punishment of crime, and reward of virtue. If a citizen will not come forward in the defence of the country from an inward feeling of his duty, let him be either allured by rewards or compelled by force. If people have no longer a sense of the intrinsic value of justice; if they no longer acknowledge that uprightness of life and dealing is true happiness, let injustice be corrected; let fraud be punished. In this manner, it is true, the state gains the object of society only by half.

External motives do not render him happy on whom they do nevertheless act. He who eschewed fraud from love of honesty, is far happier than he who only dreads the arbitrary penalty which the state attaches to fraud; but to his fellowman, it is of little consequence from what motives evil-doing is refrained from, or by what means his rights and property are secured to him. The country is defended all the same, whether the citizen fight for it from patriotism, or from fear of positive punishment; although the citizen himself is happy in the former case, and unhappy in the latter. If the internal happiness of society cannot be entirely preserved, at least, external peace and security must, at any rate, be enforced.

Accordingly, the state is, if need be, contented with dead works, with services without spirit, with consonance of action without consonance of thought. Even he, who thinks nothing of laws, must do as the law bids, when once it has been sanctioned. The individual citizen may be allowed the privilege of judging of the laws, but not that of acting up to his judgment; for, as a member of society, he was obliged to surrender that right, because without such surrender, a social compact would be a chimera. Not so religion! Religion knows of no actions without persuasion, of no works without spirit, of no consonance of acting without consonance of thought. Religious observances without religious thoughts, are idle boys' play, and no worship; this, as such, must, therefore, proceed from the spirit, and can neither be purchased by rewards, nor enforced by punishments. But from civil actions also religion withdraws its auspices, so far as they are not produced by principle, but by authority. Nor has the state to expect any further co-operation of religion, when it cannot act otherwise than by rewards and punishments; for when that is the case, the duties towards God cease to be of any consideration; and the relations between man and his creator have no effect. All the help religion can then lend the state, consists in teaching and comforting. It instills, by its divine lessons, into the citizen, principles tending to public utility; and, with its superhuman consolations, supports the malefactor doomed to die for the public good.

Here there already appears an essential difference between the state and religion. The state dictates and coerces; religion teaches and persuades. The state enacts laws; religion gives commandments. The state is armed with physical force, and makes use of it, if need be; the force of religion is love and benevolence. The former renounces the undutiful, and thrusts him out; the latter receives him in its bosom, and yet in the last moments of his present life, tries, not quite unavailingly, to instruct, or, at least, to console him. In one word; civil society, as a moral entity, may have compulsory power; nay, was actually invested with it by the social compact; religious society lays no claim to it; nor can all the compacts in the world confer it on it. The state possesses perfect rights; the church, only imperfect rights. In order to place this in a proper light, I must beg leave to remount to primary ideas, and to enquire more narrowly into

The Origin of Compulsory Rights, and the Validity of Covenants amongst Mankind.

I know I risk becoming too speculative for many a reader. But is not every one at liberty to pass over what does not suit his taste? To the curious in the law of nature, it may not be uninteresting to see in what manner I sought to define the first principles thereof.

The quality (moral power) of making use of any thing whatsoever as a means of one's happiness, is called a right. But the power itself is called moral, when it consists with the laws of wisdom and goodness; and the things which may serve as the means of happiness, are called goods. Man has, therefore, a right to certain goods or means of happiness, so far as that right is not inconsistent with the laws of wisdom and goodness.

That, which according to the laws of wisdom and goodness, must be done, or that of which the reverse would be contrary to the laws of wisdom and goodness, is called morally necessary. The moral necessity (obligation) of doing or forbearing, is called a duty.

The laws of wisdom and goodness cannot oppose one another. If I have a right to do something, my neighbour can have no right to hinder me; else one and the same action would be both morally possible and morally impossible. To every right, therefore, there answers a duty. The duty of forbearing to hinder, answers the right of acting; the duty of performing, the right of demanding, and so on.[6]

Wisdom combined with goodness, is called justice. The law of justice on which a right is founded, is either of a nature, that all the conditions on which the predicate belongs to the subject are given to the holder of the right, or it is not. In the former case, it is a perfect, in the latter, an imperfect right; namely, with an imperfect right, part of the conditions on which it is due, depend on the knowledge and conscience of the duty-bounden; he too, therefore, is, in the former case, perfectly bound to discharge the duty which answers that right, but in the latter, only imperfectly. There are perfect and imperfect duties as well as perfect and imperfect rights; those are called compulsory rights and compulsory duties; these, on the contrary, are termed pretensions, petitions, conscientious duties. Those are external, these internal. Compulsory rights may be enforced; but petitions may be dismissed. To forbear discharging compulsory duties, is wrong and unjust; whereas the omission of conscientious duties is only unconscionableness.

The goods to which man has an exclusive right are, 1, his personal abilities; 2, whatsoever he brings forth by them, and the well doing of which he promotes; whatsoever he cultivates, breeds, protects, &c., (the fruits of his industry); 3, goods of nature, which he has so united with the fruits of his industry, that they can no longer be sundered from them without damage, which, therefore, he has made his own. Accordingly, in this consists his natural property. Even in the state of nature, and yet before any compact whatsoever was entered into by mankind, those objects were exempted from the general communion of goods; namely, men originally held only such goods in common, as were produced by nature, without any one's industry or co-operation. Not all property is merely conventional.

Without beneficence man cannot enjoy happiness, not only without passive, but equally as little without active beneficence. He can become perfect no otherwise than by mutual assistance; by an interchange of kind offices, and by both an active and passive union with his fellowmen.

Therefore, when man possesses goods, or has at his command means which he can spare, that is, which are not necessary for his own existence, or of use for his *Meliority*, he is in duty bound to employ part thereof for the good of his fellow men, i. e., in beneficence; for meliority is inseparable from beneficence.

But for the same reasons, he, too, has a right to the beneficence of his fellow-men. He may expect, and pretend that others shall relieve him with their spare goods, and co-operate in his perfection. Only let it be always remembered what we mean by the word "Goods;" viz. all internal and external powers of man, so far as they may become the means of happiness to himself and others. Accordingly, every thing man, in the state of nature, possesses of industry, substance and ability, every thing he can call his, is dedicated partly to his own use (private interest), partly to beneficence.

However, as man's means are limited, and therefore, exhaustible, the same means or goods may, at times, not serve for myself and my fellow-men at once. Neither can I employ those goods or means on behalf of all my fellow-creatures, nor at all times, nor under all circumstances. And as I am bound to make the best possible use of my powers; the quantum, object, time and circumstance of my beneficence will depend on an election, and more precise determination.

By whom is this to be decided? By whom are cases of collision to be adjusted? Not by my neighbour; for to him not all the grounds are given on which the conflict of duties must be decided. Besides, every one else would have the same right; and if every one of my fellow-creatures should decide in his own favour, as most probably he would, the difficulty would not be removed.

To me, and to me alone, therefore, belongs, in a state of nature, the right of determining whether, to what extent, when, to whom, and under what circumstances I am bound to exercise beneficence. Nor can I, in a state of nature, at any time, be forced to beneficence by coercive means. My duty to be beneficent is only a conscientious duty, of which, externally, I have to render no account to any body; so is my right to my neighbour's beneficence, only a right of petitioning, which may be met with a refusal. In a state of nature, all positive duties of men to one another, are only imperfect duties, the same as their positive rights over one another, are imperfect rights, no duties which may be insisted upon, no rights which warrant coercion. In a state of nature, the duties and rights of forbearing only are perfect. I am perfectly in duty bound, no to wrong any one, and perfectly justified in preventing any one from wronging me. Now wronging, every one knows, means acting against the perfect right of another.

It may, indeed, be supposed that the duty of making reparation, is a positive duty to which man is bound even in a state of nature. When I have caused damage to my neighbour, I am, without any compact, and solely by the laws of natural justice, bound to make it good to him, and he may compel me to do so.

But although making reparation, certainly, is a positive act; the obligation to it, in the main, arises from the forbearing duty, not to wrong. For the damage which I cause my neighbour, as long as the effects of it are not removed, must be considered a protracted injury. Therefore, all the while that I omit making it good, I am violating a negative duty, for I continue to wrong. Accordingly, the duty of making reparation forms no exception of the rule, that in a state of nature, man is independent, or that he is not positively under obligation to any one. No one has a compulsory right to dictate to me, how much of my own I am to employ on behalf of others, or to whom I am to give the benefit of it. It must depend entirely on my discretion, by what rule cases of collision are to be decided.

Nor is the natural relation of parents to their children, any ways contrary to this general law of nature. It will easily be conceived, that in a state of nature, those only are independent, who are thought able of rationally deciding cases of collision. Therefore, before children have arrived at the age, when they may be supposed to have the full use of reason, they have no claim to independence; but must let others decide for them, in what manner, and for what purpose, they are to employ their powers and abilities. But parents, on their part, are bound to inure their children to the art of deciding cases of collision; and also, as they increase in judgment, to allow them, step by step, the free and independent use of their powers and abilities.

Now, in a state of nature, it is true, even parents are, in certain respects, externally under obligation to their children; and those might be thought positive duties, which can be enforced even without any compact, by the mere laws of wisdom and goodness. Yet, methinks, that in a state of nature, the right of enforcing the training of the children belongs to the parents reciprocally, and to no third person, who, befriending the former, should want to compel the latter to train them. But that parents have that compulsory right over one another, arises from the agreement they are supposed to have entered into, although not by word of mouth, still by the act itself.

Whoever co-operates in producing a being fit for enjoying happiness, is, by the law of nature, bound to promote its happiness as long as it is not itself able to attend to its own well-doing. This is the natural duty of training: abstractedly, it is true, a conscientious duty; but by the act itself, the parents have agreed to assist one another in it, or to conjointly discharge that duty. In a word, by cohabitation itself, they entered the matrimonial state; and, at the same time, into a tacit agreement to conjointly qualify for happiness, the being destined to happiness, which they produce; that is, to train it.

From this principle, all the duties and rights of matrimony very naturally flow; and there is no need to adopt, as professors of law are wont, a double principle, whence to deduce them. The duty to train children follows from the agreement to beget them; and the obligation of domesticating together, from the duty of training. Marriage, therefore, is, in the main, nothing but an agreement between persons of different sexes, to jointly bring children into the world; and on this rests the whole system of their duties and rights.[7] But that mankind by agreement, leave the state of nature, and enter that of society, will be shown further on. Accordingly, neither the parent's duty to train their children, although, in certain respects, it may be called compulsory, forms an exception from the mentioned law of nature: that in a state of nature, man is independent; and that to him alone belongs the right of deciding cases of collision between private use and beneficence.

In this light consists the natural liberty of man, which constitutes a great portion of his happiness. Independence, therefore is included in the goods exclusively his, and which he is qualified to employ as a means of his happiness; and whoever hinders him in it, injures him, and commits injustice. Man, in a state of nature, has the control over all that is his; over the free use of his powers and abilities, the free use of whatever he thereby produced (the fruits of his industry), or of what he united in an inseparable manner with the fruits of his industry; and it depends on him, how much of what he can spare of those goods, he shall give up for the benefit of his fellow-men, when, and to whom he shall give it up. All his fellow-men have only an imperfect right to his superfluity, the right of petitioning; and his, the absolute owner's conscientious duty it is, to dedicate part of his goods to beneficence; nay, at times, he is bound to sacrifice to it even his private interest, in so far as beneficence renders happier than selfishness, provided the sacrifice be made from a free will, and from a spontaneous impulse. All this appears plain enough; but I will go yet a step farther.

When that independent man has once passed judgment, that judgment must stand good. In a state of nature, when I have made up my mind, to whom I shall give up part of my own, how much of it, and when shall I give it up: when I have sufficiently declared this, my voluntary determination, and my neighbour, in whose favour it was taken, accepts the good; if my right of deciding have any meaning at all, the transaction must be of force and effect. If my decisions be powerless, and leave things *in statu quo*; if, in respect to the right, it produce not the change I determined upon, my supposed quality of passing judgment involves a palpable contradiction. My decision must, therefore, operate; it must alter the condition of the right. The good in question must cease to be mine, and have actually become my neighbour's. By that transaction, my neighbour's right, till now imperfect, must have become a perfect right, the same as my own once perfect right must have been transformed into an imperfect right; else my decision would be a mere cypher. Therefore, after the transaction is over, I can no longer claim the surrendered good without injustice. If I do, I injure; I act against the perfect right of my neighbour.

This holds good as well of material, moveable goods, which admit of being transmitted and taken possession of by hands, as of immoveable, or even spiritual goods, the right to which can be resigned and accepted by a sufficient declaration of the will only. In the main, every thing depends upon that declaration of the will; and even the actual transmission of moveable goods, can only be valid as far as it is considered a token of a sufficient declaration of the will. The mere transmission, considered by itself, neither gives nor takes away a right, whenever that intention is not coupled with it. What I put in my neighbour's hand, I have not, therefore, transmitted to him; and what I take out of his hand, I have not thereby yet legally accepted, if I have not signified that the transaction has taken place with that intention. But if transmission, merely as a token, be valid, other significant tokens may be substituted for it, with such goods as do not admit of a real transmission. We may, therefore, resign and surrender to others, our right to immoveable or even spiritual goods, by sufficiently intelligible tokens.

In this manner, property may pass from one to another. What I have made my own by my industry becomes, through cession, the goods of another, which I cannot again take away from him without committing an act of injustice.

One step more, and the validity of covenants is placed on a solid foundation. The right of deciding cases of collision, is itself, as shown above, an *incorporeal* good of independent man, so far as it may become to him a means of happiness. In a state of nature, every man has a perfect, and his neighbour an imperfect, right to the use of this means. But as, at least, in many cases, the use of that right is not absolutely necessary for support, it is a superfluous good, which, as already demonstrated, may be resigned and surrendered to others, by a sufficient declaration of the will. The act by which this is done, is called a promise, and when joined on the other side by acceptance, that is, when an assent to such transfer of rights is sufficiently signified, a covenant arises. Consequently, a covenant is nothing but, on the one side, the surrender, and on the other, the acceptance of the right of deciding cases of collision about certain goods superfluous to the promiser.

According to what has been proved above, such a covenant must be kept. The right of deciding, which previously formed part of my goods, that is, which was mine, has, by that cession, become the good of my neighbour, that is his; and I cannot again take it away from him without offending. The pretension which he, as well as every one else, had to the use of this my independence, so far as it is not absolutely necessary for my support, has, by that act, passed into a perfect right, which he is qualified to assert by forcible means. This result is incontestable, if my right of deciding is at all to have force and effect.[8]

I leave off my speculative contemplations, and turn again into my former track. But first I shall establish the conditions on which, according to the above principles, a covenant is valid, and must be kept.

1. Caius possesses a good (some means or other of happiness; the use of his personal abilities themselves, or the right to the fruits of his industry, and the goods of nature united therewith, or whatsoever else became his own in a rightful manner, be it corporeal, or incorporeal: privileges immunities, and the like).

2. But that good is not- indispensably required for his support, and may therefore be employed on behalf of beneficence, that is, for the benefit of others.

3. Sempronius has an imperfect right to that good; he, as well as every one else, may petition, but not compel its present application to his own use. The right to decide belongs to Caius; it is his, and he cannot be deprived of it by force.

4. Caius makes use of his perfect right, decides in favour of Sempronius, and declares his will by intelligible tokens, that is, Caius promises.

5. Sempronius accepts, and likewise expresses his assent, in a sufficiently significant manner.

Thus Caius's decision is effective, and of force; that is, the good which was the property of Caius has, in virtue of that transaction, become the property of Sempronius. Caius's perfect right has passed into an imperfect one; the same as Sempronius's imperfect right has been transformed into a perfect and compulsory one.

Caius must keep his legal promise; and in case of resistance, Sempronius can compel him to it by force.

It is by agreements of this kind, that man leaves the state of nature and joins the social union; and his own nature impels him to engage in various associations, in order to transform his precarious rights and duties into something more stable and determined. The savage only cleaves like the brute animal to the enjoyment of the present moment. Civilized man lives for the future as well, and will have something to look to also in the next moment. The very impulse of procreation — if it be not altogether animal instinct — necessitates him, as we have seen above, to form a social compact, of which we discover something analogous even amongst several species of the brute creation.

Let us proceed to the application of this theory of rights, duties, and covenants, to the difference between church and state, from which we set off. Both church and state have actions as well as persuasions for their object; those, so far as they are referable to the relation of man to man; these, so far as they are referable to the relation of nature to God. Men have need of one another; they hope for and promise, render services to, and expect them in return from one another. The miscellany of abundance and scarcity, strength and infirmity, selfishness and liberality, dispensated to them by nature, urges them to enter into a social union, to the end of giving a wider scope to their powers and emergencies. Every individual is obligated to apply to the good of the united society, a share of his abilities and the rights thereby acquired. But what share is he to apply so? "When and for what purpose is he to apply it? Abstractedly, all this should be decided by the contributor only? but they may also think proper to renounce that right of independence, by a social compact, and to transform by positive laws, those imperfect duties into perfect ones; that is, they may agree upon and fix a nearer rate of how much of his rights every member may be lawfully forced to apply to the benefit of society. The state, or whoever represents it, is imagined as a moral person who is set over those rights. The state, therefore, has rights and a jurisdiction over the goods and acts of man; it may, in a lawful manner, give and take, order and forbid; and because its object is also actions, as such, it may likewise reward and punish. I acquit myself externally of my duty to my neighbour, when I render him his due; the action may on my part be enforced or voluntary. Now when the state cannot operate by means of internal motives, and thereby provide for me too, it at least operates by external ones, and sees justice done to my neighbour.

Not so the Church. She is founded on the relation between God and man. God is no being who needs our beneficence, who requires our assistance, who claims any of our rights for his use, or whose own rights can ever become embroiled and in conflict with ours. The (in more than one respect) unfit division of duties, in duty to God, and in duty to man, could not but lead to those erroneous ideas. The parallel has been drawn too far. To God — to man: thought they. From duty to our neighbour we sacrifice, and give up part of what is ours, so we do from duty to God. Men desire services; so does God. My duty to myself may come in collision and conflict with my duty to my neighbour; so it may with my duty to God. It is not that every one will fall in with those absurd propositions, when put to him in dry words; yet every one has more or less imbibed them, and infected his blood with them. It is from that source, that all the usurpation flowed, which (so styled) ministers of religion indulged themselves in, under the designation of Church; all the violence and persecution they practised — all the feuds and discord, all the mutiny and sedition they fomented; and all the evils, which time out of mind, were caused under the cloak of religion, by its fiercest foes, hypocrisy and misanthropy, are wholly and solely the result of that pitiful sophism, that insinuation of a conflict between God and man, between the rights of the Godhead and the rights of mortals.

In the system of man's duties, the duties to God, in the main, form no distinct division. All the duties of man are duties to God, some concern ourselves, some our neighbours. Out of love of God we are rationally to love ourselves, his creatures; out of rational love of ourselves we are bound to love our neighbours.

The system of our duties rests on a twofold principle, on man's relation to nature; and on the creatures relation to the creator. The former is Moral philosophy, the latter. Religion; and with him who is convinced of the truth, that the relations of nature are nothing else but expressions of the Divine Will, those two principles flow into one; to him the ethics of reason are sacred like religion. Nor does religion, or the relation between God and man, require of us any other duties; it only gives those same duties and obligations a sublimer sanction. God does not want our assistance, desires no service of us,[9] no sacrifice of our rights for his benefit, no surrender of our independence in his advantage. His rights can never clash or become embroiled with ours. He only designs our good, the good of every individual; and that surely must consist with itself, and cannot contradict itself.

This common-place is so trite, that good sense is surprised that people could ever have been of a different opinion. And yet mankind have, from the beginning, acted against those plain principles! Well will it be for them, if in the year 2240 they leave off doing so.

The next conclusion to be drawn from those maxims, methinks, is that the Church has no rights over goods or property, no claim to contributions or cessions; that her privileges can never interfere with ours; and that therefore there never can occur a case of collision between her and the citizens. Since then it is thus, no covenant either can take place between them, for all covenants suppose cases of collision to be adjusted. Where there are no imperfect rights no collisions of claims can arise; and when there is not claim against claim to be decided, a covenant is a chimera.

Not all human compacts could therefore give the Church rights over goods or property, because from her nature, she can neither claim nor possess an imperfect right over either. No compulsory right can therefore ever belong to her, nor can any compulsory duty to her be ever imposed on her members. All the rights the Church has, are to exhort, instruct, fortify and console; and the duties of the citizen consist in an inclined ear, and a docile heart.[10] Nor has the Church a right to punish actions. Civil actions are of the province of the civil government, and proper religious actions, from their nature, admit neither of coercion nor bribery; they either arise from a spontaneous impulse of the mind, or are idle play and repugnant to the true spirit of religion.

But when the Church has no estate of her own, who is to pay the teachers of religion? Who is to remunerate the preachers of the fear of God? Religion and wages — lessons of virtue and pay — sermons of piety and remuneration. Those ideas seem to shun one another. What effect does a teacher of wisdom and virtue hope of his labors, while he is receiving pay, and selling himself to the highest bidder? What impression does a preacher of piety expect to make, while he is working for wages? "Behold," says Moses, "I have taught you statutes and judgments, even as the Lord my God commanded me, &c."[11] "As the Lord my God, &c. the Rabbins interpret: gratuitously, "Even so I teach you, and so are you to teach yours." Paying, hiring, &c. is so unnatural to that exalted occupation, so irreconcilable to the manners which it requires, that the least love of lucre or money-making seems to degrade the order. A desire after riches, which we willingly forgive any other class, seems to us in that, avarice and greediness, or actually very soon degenerates into avarice and greediness with men who devote themselves to that noble occupation, because it is so unnatural to their calling. A compensation for loss of time is the utmost that can be granted them; and the fixing and giving it, is the business of the State not of the Church. What has the Church to do with things that are for sale, that are bargained and paid for? Time constitutes a part of our property, and he who employs his for the good of the public, has a right to expect to be compensated out of the public purse. The Church compensates not; religion buys nothing, pays for nothing, and allows no wages.

These, methinks, are the boundary lines between Church and State, so far as both have an influence on the actions of man. In respect to persuasions they come rather nearer to one another; for there the State has no other means of operating but the Church. Both must instruct, advise, animate, induce; but neither reward nor punish, neither force nor bribe: for even the State could not acquire, by any compact whatsoever, the least control over persuasions. Generally speaking, man's persuasions know nothing of beneficence, and admit of no control, I cannot renounce my persuasion as such out of love to my neighbour; I cannot, out of beneficence, surrender and make over to him a share of my own judgment; and as little can I assume, or in any way acquire a control over his persuasions. The right to our persuasions is unalienable, and cannot pass from one person to another; for it neither gives nor supersedes any claim to property, good, or franchise. Accordingly, the least preference which you publicly give to one of your own religion and opinion, may be called an indirect bribe; the smallest privilege you withhold from dissenters,[12] indirect penalty, which, in the main, tends to the same effect as a direct premium for acquiescing, and a direct fine for resisting. The distinction between premium and privilege, between fine and restriction, so much insisted upon in some textbooks of Canon law, is but a paltry delusion. The remark may be of use to the grammarian; but to the unfortunate, who must not participate in the rights of man, because he cannot say: "I believe," when he does not believe; because he will not be a Christian on his tongue, and a Jew in his heart, that distinction affords a sorry consolation. Besides; which are the limits of privilege on the one side, and restriction on the other? With moderate skill in dialectics, one may enlarge those ideas, and keep stretching them, until they become, on the one side, civil happiness; and, on the other, oppression, persecution, and exile.

Fear and hope work on man's instinct of desiring; reasoning on his judging faculty. You are making use of the wrong means, when you want to lead man, by fear or hope, to adopt or reject certain dogmas. And although that may not be directly your object, still you spoil your better designs, if you do not remove fear and hope as far away as possible. You are bribing and deluding your own heart, or your heart is deluding you, when you believe that a test of truth can subsist; that freedom of enquiry can remain uninjured, while here, consideration and dignities await the inquirer; and there, contumely and indigence. Remonstrances of good or evil are instruments for working on the will; those of truth or untruth, for working on the understanding. Let him who wants to work on the understanding, first of all lay aside the former instruments; else he will be in danger of unintentionally planning, where he should cut right through; of fastening, where he should break up.

Then, which is the best form of government to be recommended to the Church? None, — Who is to decide when disputes arise about religious matters? He whom God gave the ability of convincing. What occasion is there for a government, where there is nothing to govern? for a supreme magistracy, where no one needs to be a subject? for the judicial office, where cases of contested rights or claims can never occur? Neither State nor Church is a competent judge in theological matters; for the members of society could not concede that right to either by any compact whatsoever. The State, it is true, is, from a distance, to take care that no doctrines be propagated, which do not consist with public decency, no doctrines which, like atheism and epicurism, sap the foundation of civil society. Plutarch and Bayle may, if they please, make it a subject of inquiry, whether a state may not subsist better under atheism than under superstition.'^ They may estimate and compare the troubles which have hitherto arisen to the human race from both those sources of woe, and which still threaten to arise. In the main, this is nothing more than inquiring whether a hectic or an ardent fever be the most fatal? Yet one would wish his friends neither. So every civil society will act rightly in not suffering either fanaticism or atheism to strike root and spread about. The political body sickens and is miserable all the same, whether it be eaten up by a cancer, or consumed by an ardent fever.

But it is from a distance only that the state is to give this a consideration: and it is also to favor with wise temperance, even the doctrine on which its true happiness depends, and not directly interfere with any controversy whatsoever, or seek to decide it with a high hand. For it is evidently acting against its own purpose, when it directly forbids inquiry, and lets controversies be decided otherwise than by arguments of reason. Nor is it to concern itself about all the opinions adopted or rejected, either by the established or the tolerated doctrine. The question is only of those main principles, in which all religions agree, and without which happiness is a dream, and virtue itself no longer virtue. Without a God, a Providence, and a future state, philanthropy is an inherent weakness, and beneficence little more than a pack of nonsense, into which we seek to talk one another, to the end that the simpleton may drudge, and the man of sense live luxuriously, and laugh at his expense!

It will scarce be necessary yet to touch on the question: is it allowable to swear ministers and priests to certain religious doctrines? On what should this be done? The above-mentioned fundamental articles of all religions cannot be confirmed by an oath. You must take the swearer's word for it that he admits them; else his oath is an empty sound, puffed in the air, with no greater conquest of himself than a simple declaration would cost him; for surely all the confidence in oaths, and their whole credit, rests merely on those fundamental tenets of morality. But if it be particular articles of this or that religion, to which I am to swear, or which I am to abjure; if it be principles, without which virtue and decency may all the same subsist amongst men, although the state, or those who represent it, think them ever so necessary for my eternal salvation; I ask, what right has the State thus to rake into the innermost recesses of the human heart, and force men to avowals which yield neither comfort nor profit to society? It could not have been conceded to it; for all the conditions of a covenant set forth above, are wanting here. It does not concern any of my superfluous goods, which I am to part with to my neighbour; it does not concern any object of beneficence; and cases of collision to be decided, are out of the question here. But then how can the State assume a quality which does not admit of being conceded by a covenant, which cannot pass from one to another, nor be made over by a declaration of the will? But let us, into the bargain, inquire, whether swearing to believing or not believing is a cogitable idea? whether men's opinions in general, their concurring or not concurring in abstract propositions — is a subject on which they can be sworn at all?

Oaths beget no new duties. The most solemn appeal to God in witness of truth, neither gives nor takes away a right which did not already exist without it, neither does it impose on the appellant any obligation which was not incumbent on him before. Oaths serve merely to awaken conscience, if peradventure it have fallen asleep; and to draw its attention to what the judge of the universe demands of it any how. Taking an oath, therefore, properly serves neither for a conscientious man, nor for a determined profligate. The former must know, any how — must, without oaths or self-imprecations, be penetrated with the truth that God is a witness not only of all the words and depositions of man, but of all his thoughts and most secret emotions, and that he lets not the transgression of his holy will pass over unpunished. As for the hardened unconscionable villain,

"He fears not God, who spares not man."

Accordingly, oaths are made only for the ordinary description of mortals, or, in the main, for every one of us, so far as, in many instances, we may be classed with that description; for the weak, irresolute and wavering, who have principles, but do not always act up to them — who are indolent and remiss in doing what they see and acknowledge to be right — who indulge their humors, defer, and palliate, to please some foible or other, seek for excuses, and, in most Cases, think they have found them. They purpose, but have not firmness enough to persevere in their purposes. It is they, whose will wants steeling, whose conscience must be roused. He, who stoutly denies a charge in a court, may still have the property of others in his possession, and yet not be so determinately wicked as to want to be dishonest. Perhaps he spent it, or let it go out of his hands, and, for the present, only wants to gain time by denying; and so the good genius, who fights within him the battle of virtue, is put off from day to day, until he is tired out and succumbs. We must, therefore, hasten to his assistance, and convert the case, which admits of delay, into one, which happens on the spot, in which the present moment is decisive, and all excuses fall to the ground. But then we must also summon all the awe, muster up all the force and energy, with which the recollections of God, the all righteous avenger and retributer, is apt to act on the human mind.

This is the purpose of oaths. And from this, I think it is evident, that men may be sworn only to such things as are perceptible by the external senses, to things of which they can affirm and declare the truth, with the positiveness which the evidence of the external sense carries with it: as, "I saw, I heard, received, gave, did not see;" and so on. But we are putting conscience to a cruel torture, when we question them about matters which belong to the internal sense only. Do you believe this? Are you convinced of it? Are you fully persuaded now? Do you think so too? If there still remain a doubt behind in a fold of your heart, in a nook of your mind, state it, or the Lord will avenge the using of his name in vain. For mercy's sake! spare tender conscience; if it had to maintain a thesis out of the first book of Euclid, it must, at that moment, be seized with fear, and undergo inexpressible torment.

The perceptions of the internal sense are of themselves seldom so palpable that the mind can safely hold them fast, and render them again as often as may be required. They will, at times, escape it, just when it thinks it is seizing them. About what I now think I am quite certain of, a slight doubt steals in, the next moment, and keeps lurking in a corner of my heart, without my perceiving it. Many positions for which I would suffer martyrdom to day, will perhaps appear very problematical to me to-morrow. And if I am even to render those internal perceptions by words and symbols, or to swear to words and symbols, which other men propose to me; the uncertainty will be still greater. It is impossible that I and my neighbour can unite the selfsame inward sensations to the selfsame words. For we cannot confront the former with one another, or form a comparison between them, and correct them, unless by words. We cannot define words by things, but again must have recourse to words or to symbols, and in the end to metaphors; because by that device, we, as it were, lead the conceptions of the internal sense back to external sensible impressions. But with that process, what confusion and obscurity will there not remain behind, in the signification of words? How will not the ideas vary, which different men, in different times and ages, link to the selfsame symbols and words?

Good reader! whoever yon may be, accuse me not, on that account, of a sceptical turn, or of the insidious design of making a sceptic of you. Perhaps I am one of those, who are freest from that morbidness of the mind, and who most zealously wish to be able to cure all their fellow-creatures of it. But just because I have so frequently performed that cure on myself, and tried it on others, experience taught me how difficult it is, and how little we can answer for the result. With my best friend, with whom I fancied I thought ever so congenially, I very often could not agree in philosophical and theological truths. After a long dispute and conversation, it would at times turn out, that we had each of us united a different idea with the self-same word. In not a few instances, we apprehended alike, but only expressed ourselves each in a different

53

manner: and just as often we would felicitate one another on coinciding, when, in thought, we were still wide apart from one another. And yet we were neither of us unpractised in thinking; we were both used to handle abstract ideas, and our earnest aim seemed to be alike truth, more tor the sake of truth, than of gaining the point. Notwithstanding which our ideas wanted a good deal of mutual rubbing, before they would dovetail into each other, before we could say with certainty: Now we agree. Ah, whoever has experienced this in his life-time, and can still be intolerant, can still bear his fellowman animosity, because he does not think or express himself about theological matters exactly as he himself does — him I would not have for my friend; he has entirely stripped himself of humanity.

And ye, my fellow-creatures, ye take a man, with whom, perhaps, ye never had any conversation about those matters; ye propose to him the most abstruse thesis in metaphysics and theology, clothed as they were, ages ago, in words or so-called symbols; ye make him swear by the most awful of names, that he associates with those words the very identical idea which you yourself associate with them; and that both he and you associate with them the very identical idea associated with them by him, who wrote them down ages ago; you make him swear that he subscribes to those theses, and draws none of them into question; and with this subscription on oath, you connect office and dignity, power and influence, the temptation to which, removes so many a contradiction, hushes so many a doubt. And if at any future time, the man's internal conviction prove not quite so adamantine as, to you, he pretended it was, you accuse him of the most heinous of crimes; you indict him for having forsworn himself, and you let ensue what must ensue in such a case! Now, judging with all possible lenity, is not here the measure of guilt equal on both sides?

Ay, say the more reasonable amongst ye; we do not swear the man to his creed: no, we leave conscience full freedom; and only require of a fellow-citizen, whom we are about to invest with a certain office, that he shall declare, on his oath, that the office entrusted to him, on condition of conformity, is not accepted by him without conforming. It is a contract into which we enter with him. And if, in the sequel, doubts arise, which destroy that conformity, does it not rest with him to remain true to his conscience, and resign the office? Is there any liberty of conscience, any rights of man, that warrant the breaking of a contract?

Very well! I shall not oppose to this appearance of justice, all the arguments which may be opposed to it on the self-evident principles laid down above. What is the use of needless iteration? But for humanity's sake, look at the consequences of which that custom has been hitherto productive amongst the most civilized nations. Take all the men who mount your academical chairs, and your pulpits, and still have their doubts about many an article they swear to, on accepting their appointments; take all the bishops who sit in the House of Lords, all the truly great men invested with power and dignity in England, who do not admit the thirty-nine articles quite so unconditionally as they were proposed to them. Take them all, and then still say, civil liberty cannot be granted to my oppressed nation, because they make so light of oaths! Heaven preserve me from misanthropical thoughts! At this sad reflection, they might easily get the better of me.

No! Out of regard for humanity I will, on the contrary, believe that all those men do not consider perjury that which is charged to them as such. Good sense, perhaps, tells them that neither state nor church had a right to connect office, honour and dignity, with the belief in, and swearing to, certain propositions, or to make the belief in certain propositions, the condition on which to confer them. Such condition, perhaps, they think is null of itself, because it tends to no one's good; because the breaking of it causes no deterioration of any one's right or property.[13] If, therefore, wrong have been done, and it cannot be denied that there has, it was at the time when the benefits held out to them, tempted them into so inadmissible an oath. That evil can now no longer be remedied; and it can be remedied least by resigning the office so gotten. For the sake of acquiring justifiable worldly advantages, they, at the time, certainly, used God's most holy name in a manner unjustifiable with him. But what has been so done, cannot be made undone by their resigning the fruits they enjoy of it; nay, the disorder, scandal, and other bad consequences, inevitably resulting from the throwing up of their appointment, perhaps accompanied by a formal and public declaration of the matter of dissent, might only aggravate the evil. How much more advisable would it, therefore, be to the state, to themselves, and those depending on them, to leave things undisturbed, and continue to State and Church the services for which Providence gave them talent and inclination. It is in that, that their vocation for the public ministry consists, not in what they may be thinking about immutable truths, and theoretical propositions, which, in fact, concern only themselves, and not their fellow-men. And if many a one have too tender a conscience to owe his comfort to such fine-spun apologies, those who are weak enough to yield to them, are not therefore to be condemned altogether. It is not, at any rate, willful perjury, but human frailty, with which I would tax men of their merit.

To conclude this section, I shall recapitulate the result to which I have been led by my contemplations.

The purpose of Church and State is to promote by public measures, the happiness of man both in this life and in that to come.

They both work on the persuasions and the actions of men, on principles and their application; the State, with such grounds as are resting on relations of man to man, or to nature; the Church, or the religion of the State, with such grounds as are resting on relations of man to God. The state uses man as *the immortal Son of Earth*; religion as *the image of his Creator*.

Principles are free, Persuasions, from their nature, admit neither of compulsion nor bribery; they are the business of man's judging faculty, and must be decided on by the standard of truth or untruth. Good and evil work on his approving or disapproving faculty; fear and hope govern his instincts; reward and punishment direct his will, spur his energy, animate, tempt or frighten him.

But if principles are to render happy, man must neither be terrified nor wheedled into them; the judgment of the reasoning faculties alone must stand good. To let ideas of good or evil intermeddle, is to let cases be decided by an incompetent judge.

Neither State nor Church has therefore, a right to submit the principles and persuasions of men to any compulsion whatsoever. Neither Church nor State is entitled to connect rights over persons, or claims to things with principles and persuasions; and to weaken, by extraneous admixture, the influence of the force of truth on the discerning faculty.

Not even the social compact could concede such a right to either State or Church. For compacts about objects which, from their nature, are unalienable, are intrinsically nugatory, and cancel themselves.

Nor do the most sacred oaths any way alter the nature of things here. Oaths engender no new duties; they are a mere solemn confirmation of what we are obligated to do without them, either by nature or in virtue of a covenant. Where no duty exists, the taking of an oath is a vain invocation of God, scandalous enough as it is, but of itself binding to nothing at all.

Besides a man can swear to that only which has the evidence of the external senses for it, that is, to what he *saw, heard, touched, felt or tasted.* The perceptions of the internal sense are no subject for a confirmation on oath.

Accordingly, all swearing to, as well as all swearing away, of principles and dogmas is inadmissible; and when done, notwithstanding, binds to nothing but to repentance of the blamable levity thus shown. If I now swear to an opinion, I am, for that, not the less at liberty to repudiate it the next moment. The misdeed of a vain oath has been committed, even if I retain it; and if I reject it, will it be said that I have forsworn myself?

Let it not be forgotten that, according to my principles, the state is not qualified to attach income, dignity and privilege, to certain distinct dogmas. As to what regards the public ministry, it is the duty of the state to appoint preachers able to teach wisdom and virtue, and of promulgating the wholesome truths on which the well-being of society depends. All more particular provisos and regulations must be left to the best discretion, and the conscience of the ministers themselves; as being the only way of preventing endless confusion, and collision of duties, which will betray even the virtuous into hypocrisy and moral dereliction. Not every offence against the dictates of reason remains unavenged.

But what if the harm have once been done? Here the State appoints and stipendiates a minister for preaching certain set dogmas. By-and-by, the man finds out that there are no grounds for those dogmas. What is he to do? How is he to proceed, in order to get his foot out of the gin into which an erring conscience made him run?

Here three different ways are open to him. He either locks up truth in his breast, and goes on preaching untruth, notwithstanding he knows better; or he throws up his situation without assigning a reason for it; or he openly vindicates truth, and leaves to the State what is to become of his place and salary; and what he is to suffer besides for his unconquerable love of truth.

Of those three ways, none, methinks, is under all circumstances to be absolutely condemned. I can imagine a condition, which would serve at the tribunal of the all-righteous judge, as an excuse for having continued to mix up with ours, all besides salutary promulgation of truths of general utility, an untruth hallowed by the State, perhaps from mistaken scrupulosity. I should, at any rate, beware taxing a pastor, irreproachable in other respects, with hypocrisy or Jesuitism on that account, unless I am thoroughly acquainted with his position and circumstances; nay so acquainted as perhaps no man ever was with his neighbour's position and circumstances. *Whoever takes credit for having never expressed himself on theological matters different from what he thought, either did not think at all, or has, at that very moment, a particular object in boasting of an untruth, which his own heart gainsays.*

With a view to persuasions and principles, religion and the civil government, therefore, agree; and it behoves both to avoid every appearance of compulsion or bribery; and confine themselves to teaching, exhorting, convincing, and showing the way to the right path. With a view to actions they do not. The relations between men and men demand actions merely as such; the relations between man and God demand them only so far as they bespeak certain persuasions and opinions. An act of public utility ceases not to be publicly useful, even when procured by force; whereas a religious act is religious only accordingly as it is done spontaneously, and with a proper intention.

The State may therefore enforce acts of public utility; reward, punish, dispense offices, posts of honor, ignominy and banishment, in order to move men to actions, of which the intrinsic value will not operate forcibly enough on their minds. The completest right and power to do so, therefore even was — and must have been — granted to it by the social compact. The State is, therefore, a moral entity, which possesses goods and privileges of its own, and may dispose of them as it pleases.

Divine religion is far from being all this; it conducts itself towards actions no otherwise than towards persuasions, because it commands actions merely as tokens of persuasions. It is also a moral entity; but its rights do not know what compulsion is. It drives not with a rod of iron, but on the contrary, leads by the strings of loving-kindness. It draws no avenging sword, dispenses no temporal goods, assumes no claim on earthly possessions, no external control over any mind. The weapons it uses are grounds and convictions; its power lays in the divine force of truth. The punishments it threatens, are the same as the rewards it holds out, — effects of kindness, salutary and beneficial even to him who receives them. By these characteristics, I know thee, daughter of the Godhead, Religion — who art in truth alone, the saving one on earth as in heaven!

The right of proscribing and banishing, which the State, at times, may think fit to exercise, is straight contrary to the spirit of religion. Excommunicate, exclude, turn away a brother, who wants to join me in my devotions, and raise his heart up to God, along with mine, in salutary participation! And that while religion denies itself the power of inflicting arbitrary punishments, least of all that torment of the soul, which he alone feels who has really religion! Pass in review all the unfortunates, that ever were to be amended by anathema and threats of damnation. Reader, whichever external church, synagogue, or mosque you may belong to; inquire and see whether you shall not discover more true religion amongst the multitude of the anathematized, than amongst the incomparably greater multitude of those who anathematized them. Now anathema is either attended with civil consequences, or it is not. If it draws on civil misery, its hardship falls on the magnanimous individual only, who considers that sacrifice due to divine truth. He who has no religion, must be out of his senses, if he expose himself to the least risk, for the sake of a supposititious truth. But if the consequences of anathema be merely of a spiritual nature (as some would fain persuade themselves they are), they again bear heavy on him only who still is susceptible of that kind of feeling. The irreligious man laughs at anathema, and continues as obdurate as ever.

And is there a possibility of completely severing anathema from civil consequences? I think I have truly observed in another place, that the introducing of ecclesiastical discipline without injuring civil happiness, resembles the answer of the Most High Judge to the Accuser: "He is in thy hands; but spare his life!" or as the commentators remark: "Demolish the cask, but let not the wine run out." Where is the anathema, where the excommunication, that can be said to be entirely without civil consequences, without influence, at least, on the civil esteem or the good name of the anathematized, the confidence he enjoys among his fellow-citizens, in default of which no one can follow his business, and be useful to his fellow-creatures, that is, be civilly happy?

But they will still appeal to the law of nature. "Every society," say they, "has a right of expelling; why should a religious society not have it too?"

I reply: "this is just where a religious society forms an exception." By virtue of a higher law, no society can exercise a right, which goes right against the main object of the institution of society itself. Excommunicating a dissenter, expelling him from the church, (says a worthy divine of this city,) is like forbidding a sick man the dispensary. Indeed, the most essential object of religious societies is common edification. We want to transport, by the magic power of sympathy, truth out of the mind into the heart; and by participation, revive to lofty perceptions, knowledge of reason, at times dead. When the heart cleaves too fast to sensual desires to hearken to reason; when it is on the point of luring reason itself with it into the snare; it must here be seized with the awe of piety, inflamed with the ardour of devotion, and learn to know pleasures of a higher order, which outweigh those of the senses, even already here on earth. And ye will repulse, at the door, the patient who most needs that medicine, who needs it the more, the less he is conscious of the want of it, and in his own conceit imagines himself to be in good health! Ought it not rather to be your first endeavour to restore to him that feeling, and recall to life the part of his soul, which is as it were, threatened with mortification? Instead of which, you deny him all assistance, and suffer the lingerer to die a moral death, from which perhaps, you might rescue him.

A certain philosopher at Athens, acted far nobler, and more according to the purpose of his school. An epicure came away from the banquet, his senses clouded by the night's revels, and his brow enwreathed with roses. He steps into the auditory of the stoics, in order to treat himself, yet at the morning-hour, with the finishing sport of enervated rakes, the sport of scoffing. The philosopher lets him alone, redoubles the fire of his eloquence against the seductions of voluptuousness, and paints the felicity of virtue with most irresistible force. The disciple of Epicurus listens, waxes attentive, casts down his eyes, tears the wreaths from his brow, and becomes himself a follower of the Stoa.

SECTION II.

Mr. Dohm's excellent work "On the Civil Melioration of the Jews," occasioned the enquiry: How far may a colony be indulged in the administration of their own laws in ecclesiastical and civil matters, in general; and in the right of anathematizing and excommunicating, in particular? Lawful power of the church — the right of anathematizing. If the colony have it at all, they must have been, as it were, enfeoffed with it, either by the state, or by the mother-church. Some one possessing those rights, in virtue of the social compact, must have given up, and transferred to them a certain portion thereof, so far as concerned themselves. But how is it if no one ever can possess such a right? if no compulsory power in theological matters belong to the mother church herself, or to the state either? — if, according to reason, the divineness which we must all acknowledge, neither the state nor the church are qualified to assume, in theological matters, any part but that of instructing; any power but that of persuading; any discipline but that of reason and principle. If this can be demonstrated, and rendered evident to the human understanding, no express covenant, and still less consuetude or prescription, are powerful enough to maintain a right that runs counter to reason; then all ecclesiastical restraint is unlawful, all external authority in theological matters, usurpation; and if it be so, the mother church neither can nor may bestow a right which does not belong to her herself, nor yet dispose of an authority which she has wrongly assumed. It may be, that, through some prevailing prejudice or other, abuses have so spread, so deeply rooted in the minds of men, that it would not be feasible or even advisable to abolish them at once, and without cautious preparation. But, in that case, it is at least our duty to counteract them from a distance; and, in the first place, throw up a dam against their further incursion. If we cannot totally eradicate an evil, we ought, at any rate, to cut off its roots.

Such was the result of my contemplations; and I ventured to lay my thoughts before the public for their opinion;[14] although I could not then state my grounds so completely as has been done since in the preceding section.

I have the happiness to live in a country in which these, my ideas, are neither novel, nor considered particularly singular. From the beginning of his reign, it has been the constant practice of the monarch by whom it is governed, to establish mankind in their full rights, with respect to religious matters. He is the first amongst the regents of our age, by whom the wise maxim: "Men are born for each other: teach thy neighbour, or bear with him,"[15] has never been lost sight of. He, indeed, with wise moderation, spared the privileges of external religion, such as he found it in possession of. It will, perhaps, require yet ages of cultivation and of preparation, before men shall comprehend, that privileges on account of religion are neither lawful, nor, in the main, useful; and that, therefore, a final removal of civil disabilities, on account of religion, would actually be a benefit. However, under that philosopher's administration, the nation has got so used to toleration and socialness in religious affairs, that the terms "Anathema," and "Excommunication" have, at least ceased to be popular ones.

However, what every just man must rejoice at, is the earnestness and zeal with which several worthy members of the Christian clergy are endeavouring to propagate amongst the people, those principles of reason, or rather of true religion; nay, some of them had no hesitation in concurring with me in my arguments against the widely worshipped idol — ecclesiastical law, and in publicly approving of the conclusion drawn from those arguments. What high notions those men must have of their vocation, that they are so willing to remove from it all by-ends! What noble confidence they must place in the force of truth, that they undertake to place it safe on its own pedestal, without any other support! Although we should differ ever so much in principles, I cannot forbear expressing my entire admiration and veneration of them, and of those noble sentiments.

Many others, readers as well as critics, bore themselves very singularly, on that occasion. They did not, indeed, controvert my arguments; on the contrary, they admitted them. None of them tried to show the least connexion between doctrine and privilege. None of them pointed out an inaccuracy in the syllogism, that my assenting or not assenting to certain immutable truths, neither gives me, nor takes away from me, any right or qualification whatsoever, nor yet authorises me to command men's means and minds at my own will and pleasure. And yet the inevitable result thereof made them startle, as at a sudden spectre. "What," cried they, "then there is no such thing as ecclesiastical law! Then all that so many doctors, and, perhaps, we ourselves, have written, read, heard, and disputed on — law, rested on a hollow foundation!" That seemed to them, going rather too far. And yet, unless there be a hidden error in the syllogism, the conclusion must necessarily be right.

The Reviewer, in the Göttingen Advertiser, quoting my assertion, "That there exists no right over persons or things, which is connected with doctrine; and that all the compacts and agreements in the world, could not make such a right possible," adds: "all this is new and hard. First principles are denied away, and there is an end to all argument."

To be sure, it concerns first principles, which are refused to be admitted. But is there, therefore, to be an end to all arguments? Are principles then never to be doubted? So men of the Pythagorean school, will be everlastingly debating about the manner in which their teacher came by his golden thigh, if no one be permitted to investigate, whether Pythagoras really had such a thing as a golden thigh.

Every game has its laws, every race or match its rules, conformably to which the umpires decide. If you want to win the stake, or carry the prize, you 'must at once acknowledge those laws and rules. Whereas, he who wants to con- template the theory of games and matches, may, by all means, have his doubts as to the fundamental principles. It is the same in a court of justice. A judge elicited from a murderer the confession of his guilt. But at the same time, the contumacious fellow maintained that he knew no reason, why it should not be just as much allowed to kill a man, for his own benefit, as to slay a beast. To him the judge might justly reply: "You deny the first principles, fellow; so there is an end to all arguing with you: anyhow you will admit that we, too, are allowed to rid the earth of such a miscreant as you, for our own benefit." But the priest, who had to prepare that felon for death, must not answer him in that manner. It was his duty to engage with him about the principles themselves, and to endeavour to remove his doubts, if he entertained them in earnest. Nor is it any otherwise in the arts and sciences. In every one of them there are certain fundamental ideas supposed, which are no further accounted for. Yet, there is not in the whole circle of human knowledge, a single point, which is superior to all doubt, not an iota which is not amenable to investigation. If my doubt lie out of the province of one forum, I must be referred to another; but I must be heard and set to rights somewhere.

Moreover, the case put by the Göttingen Reviewer (by way of an instance) to refute me, is not one in point. "Let us, however," says he, "apply those denied first principles, to a definitive case, viz.: The Jewish congregation at Berlin appoint a person to circumcise male children conformably to the precept of their religion. In virtue of that transaction, such person acquires a right to a fixed salary, to a certain rank in the congregation &c. By-and-by he is seized with scruples about the dogma or law of circumcision, and refuses to perform the operation stipulated in the contract. Will he be suffered to continue to enjoy the rights acquired by the same? And so everywhere.

How everywhere? I will admit the possibility of the thing, which, I trust, will never occur.[16] What is this case, placed so near home to me, to prove? Surely not that, according to reason, rights over persons or goods are connected with doctrines or depending on them, not that positive laws and covenants may render such rights possible. According to the reviewer's own statement, the whole depends on those two circumstances; and yet neither of them takes place in the simulated case: for the circumciser would receive a fixed salary, and enjoy a certain rank, not for his absenting to the dogma of circumcision, but for his performing the operation instead of the fathers of families. Now, if his conscience will not allow him to act in that capacity any longer, he will, by all means, have to renounce the remuneration for which he stipulated on undertaking it. But what has that in common with the privileges granted to a person because he subscribes to this or that doctrine, because he admits or rejects this or that immutable truth? All to which the simulated case may bear some analogy, would be, if the State engage and pay ministers to preach set doctrines after a certain method, and no other; and those ministers afterwards think themselves in conscience bound to deviate from the course prescribed to them. That case, which has so frequently given occasion to loud and warm disputes, I touched upon largely in the preceding section, and sought to set forth after my principles. But to me, it seems equally as little to suit the quoted simile. The reader will please to bear in mind the distinction which I established between actions required as actions, and such as are to pass merely as a token of persuasions. Here a foreskin is cut off: the circumciser may think or believe of the custom itself what he pleases; the same as a creditor, whom a court helps to recover his claim, is paid, whatever may be the debtor's notions of the obligation of paying. But how [can this be made applicable to a teacher of theological truths, whose lessons surely will bring but little profit, if his mind and heart do not agree with them, if they do not arise from his internal convictions? I signified already, in the before-mentioned place, that I would not take upon myself to prescribe to a minister, thus driven into a strait, how, as an honest man, he is to act, or to make him reproaches for having acted otherwise; and that, in my opinion, every thing depends on times, and on the circumstances and situation he may happen to be in. Who will therein presume to condemn his neighbour's conscientiousness? Who would force upon it, for so arduous a decision, a balance which, perhaps, he does not acknowledge as the true one?

That inquiry, however, does not lay exactly in my road; and has little in common with the two questions on which every thing depends, and which I shall once more repeat here.

1. Are there, according to the laws of reason, rights over persons or things, which rights are connected with dogmas, by the concurring in which they are acquired?

2. Can covenants and agreements engender perfect rights, and produce compulsory duties, where, previously, no imperfect rights and duties of conscience did not exist, independent of all covenants?

One of those two propositions must be proved by means of the law of nature, to convince me of an error. That they call my assertion new and hard, does not matter, if but truth do not contradict it. I am not, as yet, acquainted with any author who has touched upon those questions, and analysed them, in their application to ecclesiastical authority, and the right of anathematizing. They all start from the point, that there is such a thing as *Jus sacro sancto*; only every one models it in his own way, and enfeoffs with it, now an invisible person, now this or that visible one. Hobbes himself, who therein ventures to deviate farther from established notions than any one else, could not entirely divest himself of that idea. He admits of such a right, and is only seeking for a person to whom it may be entrusted with least harm. They all believe that the meteor is visible, but they have recourse to different systems for ascertaining its longitude and latitude. It would not be an unheard-of circumstance, if an unpreoccupied passenger, who just happens to look upwards at the spot where it is supposed to appear, should, with far less scholarship, prove that there is never a meteor to be seen.

I now come to a much more important objection, which has been raised to me, and which chiefly occasioned this tract. Without refuting my arguments, they again opposed to them the sacred authority of the Mosaic religion, which I profess. "What are the laws of Moses," said they, "but a system of religious government, and of the power and rights of religion?" " It may consist with reason," says an anonymous author," &c. &c. &c.[17]

That objection goes to the heart; and I must own, that, except some intemperate expressions, the ideas he gives of Judaism are the same, which even many of my brethren in the faith entertain of it. Now, could I be convinced of their being correct, I certainly would, with shame, retract my positions, and bend reason to the yoke of faith. O no! wherefore should I dissemble? If the word of God were so evidently contradictory to my understanding, the utmost I could do would be to impose silence on the latter; but my unrefuted arguments would, nevertheless, return to some secret recess of my heart, there change to harassing doubts, and those doubts would resolve into filial prayer, into fervent supplication for light. I would exclaim with the Psalmist: — "O! send me thy light, and thy truth. Let them lead me, let them bring me unto thy holy mount, and to thy residence." (Ps. xliii. 3.)

At all events, it would be hard and vexing, if, like the above anonymous writer, and him who wrote the postscript with the signature of Moerschel, the world should impute to me the scandalous design of subverting the religion which I confess, and of renouncing it, if not expressly, but, as it were, in an underhand manner. This practice of wresting meanings should be forever discarded from the conversation of the learned. *Not every one who concurs in an opinion, does, at the same time, concur in all the inferences drawn from it, though ever so correctly.* Those kinds of imputations are odious, and only Cause exasperation and pugnacity, by which truth seldom gains any thing.

Nay, the " Searcher, &c.," goes to the length of apostrophizing me in the following manner: "Or are we to presume," &c, &c.[18]

That imputation is expressed seriously and pathetically enough. But, my good sir, am I to take the step, without first considering whether it will really draw me out of the dilemma, in which, you think, I must find myself? If it be true that the corner-stones of my house are failing, and the tenement threatens to fall down, am I then right in shifting my effects from the lower story to the upper? Shall I be any safer there? Now Christianity, you know, is built on Judaism, and when this falls down, that must necessarily become one heap of ruins with it. You say, my conclusions undermine the foundation of Judaism, and you proffer me, for safety, your upper story. Must I suppose that you are mocking me? When there is the appearance of a contradiction between one truth and another, between Scripture and reason, a Christian, in earnest about "right and light," will not challenge a Jew to a controversy, but conjointly, with him, seek to discover the groundlessness of the discrepancy. Both their causes are concerned in it. Whatever else they have to settle between themselves may be deferred to another time. For the present, they must use their joint endeavours to avert the danger, and either discover the false conclusion, or show that it was nothing but a paradox which frightened them.

Thus I might now elude the snare, without engaging in any farther discussion with the "Searcher." But what would the subterfuge avail me? His compeer, Mr. Moerschel, although he does not know me personally, has seen too deep in my cards. He thinks he has discovered in the criticised preface certain marks and characteristics, by which he feels himself perfectly warranted to pronounce me as wide from the religion in which I was born and educated, as I am from the one which has been transmitted to him by his own forefathers. As a proof of this his supposition, (besides referring me to the first paragraph of my preface), he quotes from it the following passage, verbatim: "Thedoorsof the house of rational devotion," &c. &c.[19] One sees that, according to Mr. Moerschel's opinion, no believer in Revelation would so openly plead in favour of the toleration of Theists, or speak so loudly of immutable truths, taught by religion; and that a true Christian or Jew ought to pause before he calls his place of worship "the house of rational devotion." I certainly do not know what has led him to those thoughts; yet they constitute the whole superstratum of his supposition, and move him, as he expresses himself, (vol. i. p. 145,) not to invite me to embrace his own religion, or to refute it, but to intreat me, in the name and for the sake of all who revere truth, to speak resolutely and definitively of that which is, and always will be, of the first and most vital importance to the reflecting and conscientious of all religions. It is not, indeed, as he declares, his intention to make a convert of me; nor would he be the instigator of arguments and objections to the religion from which he derives genuine happiness in this life, and also expects eternal felicity in the next; and heaven knows what else the good man wants, and what he does not want. This, therefore, is to set the kind-hearted gentleman's mind at ease. I never openly controverted the Christian religion, nor will I ever engage in a controversy with any one of its sincere followers. And lest it should be again said of me, that by that declaration, I mean, as it were, to give to understand that I am very well provided with formidable weapons, wherewithal to combat that religion, if I were so inclined; might not the Jews be in possession of secret traditions, of records now become scarce and unknown, whereby historical facts would be made to appear in a light different from that in which they are represented to Christians? and more such like insinuations, which we have been thought capable of, or which were imputed to us? In order then, once for all to remove all suspicions of that kind, I herewith affirm, before the public, that I have, at least, nothing new to bring forward against the faith of the Christians; that, for ought I know, we are acquainted with no other accounts of the historical facts, and can produce no other records than those which are universally known; that I, on my part, have nothing to advance that has not been said and repeated innumerable times, by Jews and Theists, and answered over and over again by the other party. Methinks, in so many ages, and particularly in this *writative* age of ours, replies and rejoinders more than enough have been put in, in this suit. As the parties have nothing fresh to adduce, it is time the depositions were closed. He who has eyes, let him see; and he who has sense, let him examine, and live according to his convictions. What is the use of champions standing by the roadside, and offering battle to every passer-by? Discussing a matter too much does not render it any clearer, but, on the contrary, only obscures what faint glimmer of truth there may be in it. You have only to speak, write, or dispute frequently and much, for or against a proposition, be it of whatever nature it may, and rest assured, it will lose more and more of its evidence. Mr. M. need not, therefore, be under any apprehension. Through me, he certainly shall not become an occasioner of exceptions to a religion, to which so many of my fellow-creatures look for content in this life, and for unbounded felicity in the next.

I must, however, do justice to his penetrating eye. He is, partly, not wrong in his observations. It is true, *I acknowledge no immutable truths, but such as not only may be made conceivable to the human understanding, but as also admit of being demonstrated and warranted by human faculties.* There only he is misled by an erroneous notion of Judaism, when he supposes that I cannot maintain this without deviating from the religion of my forefathers. On the contrary, this is just what I hold an essential point of the Jewish religion; and I think that this doctrine forms a characteristic difference between it and the Christian. To express it in one word, I believe that Judaism knows nothing of a revealed religion, in the sense in which it is taken by Christians. The Israelites have a divine legislation: laws, judgments, statutes, rules of life, information of the will of God, and lessons how to conduct themselves in order to attain both temporal and spiritual happiness: those laws, commandments, &c., were revealed to them through Moses, in a miraculous and supernatural manner; but no dogmas, no saving truths, no general self-evident positions. Those the Lord always reveals to us, the same as to the rest of mankind, by *nature and by events*; but never in *words* or *written characters*.

I fear this will appear strange, and again be found new and hard by many readers. This distinction has always been little minded. Supernatural legislation has been taken for supernatural revelation; and Judaism was considered nothing but a sort of earlier revelation of religious propositions and tenets, necessary for the salvation of man. I shall, therefore, be obliged to explain myself somewhat largely; and lest I should be misunderstood, I will ascend to prior ideas; in order that I may set out from the same station with my readers, and keep pace with them.

We call such truths *immutable* or *eternal* as are not subject to time, but continue the same to all eternity. They are either *necessary*, immutable in and of themselves, or *casual*; that is, their perpetuity is founded either on their nature, they are true so and not otherwise, because they are cogitable so and not otherwise, or on their ideality; they are generally true, they are so and not other wise, because they became real so and not otherwise; because of all the possible truths of their kind they are the *best* so and not otherwise. In other words: necessary as well casual truths flow from a common source, from the fountain-head of all truth; the former from *reason*, the latter from the *will of God*. The propositions of necessary truths are true, because God *conceives* them so, and no otherwise;

and those of casual truths are true, because God deemed them good, and considered them to be in conformity with his wisdom so and not otherwise. The propositions of pure mathematics and logic are examples of the former kind; the general propositions of natural philosophy, pneumatology, and the laws of nature, by which the universe, the material and spiritual worlds are governed, are examples of the latter. The former are immutable even to Omnipotence, because God himself cannot make his infinite wisdom mutable; the latter, on the contrary, are subordinate to the will of God, and are immutable only so far as it pleases his holy will; that is, so far as they answer his purposes. His Omnipotence might introduce other laws instead of them; and may let exceptions take place, whenever they are of utility.

Besides those eternal truths, there also *temporal* or *historical truths*; things, which did occur at one time, and, perhaps, will never occur again. Propositions, which, through a confluence of causes and effects, have become true in one point of space and time, and which, therefore, can be conceived as true in respect to that point of space and time only. All historical truths, in their widest extent, are of that kind. Things of remote ages, which did once take place, and are narrated to us, but which we ourselves can never observe.

Those classes of truths and propositions differ no less in their nature than in respect to their means of evidence; that is, the mode and process by which men convince themselves and others of them. The doctrines of the' first class, or that of necessary truths, are founded on *reason*, that is, on an unalterable coherency, and real connexion of ideas, in virtue of which they either presuppose or exclude one another. All mathematical and logical demonstrations are of that kind. They all show the possibility or impossibility of associating certain ideas in the mind. He who would instruct his fellow-men in them, must not recommend them to his belief, but, as it were, force them on his understanding: he must not cite authorities, and appeal to the trustworthiness of men, who maintained exactly the same thing, but he must analyse the ideas in all their distinguishing characteristics, and continue to hold them up to his pupil, one by one, until his internal sense perceives their junctures and connexion. The instruction, which we may give others, in this, consists — as Socrates very justly observes — in a kind of midwifery. We cannot put any thing into their mind, which it does not actually contain already; but we may facilitate the labour it would cost them to bring to light what is hidden; that is, to render the unperceived perceivable and obvious.

The truths of the second class require, besides reason, observation as well. If we would know the laws which the Creator has prescribed to his creation, and by what general rules the mutations therein take place, we must experience, observe, and make experiments on single cases; that is, we must, in the first place, make use of the evidence of the senses; and next, educe by means of reason, out of sundry single cases, what they have in common. In doing so, we shall indeed be obliged to trust in many things, to the faith and credit of others. Our natural life does not last long enough for us to experience every thing ourselves; and we are, in many cases, necessitated to rely on credible fellowmen; and to suppose the correctness of their experience, and of the experiments they pretend to have made. But we confide in them only so far as we know, and are certain that the objects themselves still exist, and that the experiments and observations may be repeated thereon, and put to the test, by ourselves, or by those who have the opportunity and the requisite skill. Nay, when the result becomes of importance, and has a material influence on our own happiness, or on that of others, we are far less satisfied with the report of even the most creditable witnesses, who state to us their observations and experiments; but we seek an opportunity to repeat them ourselves, and to become convinced of them by their internal evidence. Thus, for instance, the Siamese may by all means believe the Europeans, when they tell them that, in their own climate, at certain seasons of the year, water becomes solid and capable of bearing heavy loads. They may take their word for it, and even go so far as to insert it in their textbooks of natural philosophy as a decided fact, on the supposition that the thing may yet be tried and ascertained. But let there be risk of life in the case; let them be desired to trust themselves or those belonging to them to the congealed element, they would not be by far so confident in the testimony of others, but first seek to convince themselves of its truth, by various observations, experiments, and trials of their own.

Historical truths, on the contrary, or those passages which, as it were, occur but once in the book of nature, must either explain themselves, or remain unintelligible; that is, they can be observed by means of the senses, only by those who are present at the time when, and at the place where they happened; every one else can only take them on authority and testimonials, while those who live at a subsequent period must absolutely depend on the authenticity of the testimonials. For the thing testified of, does no longer exist. The object itself, and the direct inspection thereof, to which perhaps an appeal would be made, are no longer found in nature. The senses cannot convince themselves of the truth. In historical matters, the narrator's reputation and his credibility constitute the only evidence. We cannot be persuaded of any historical truth, unless by testimony. Were it not for authority, the truth of history would vanish along with the events themselves.

Now, whenever it suits with God's design, that mankind shall be satisfied of any truth, his wisdom also affords them the aptest means to arrive at it. If it be a necessary truth, it grants them the degree of judgment which it requires. If a law of nature is to be promulgated to them, it inspires them with the spirit of observation; and if a fact is to be preserved to posterity, it confirms its historical certainty, and places the narrator's credibility beyond all question. I should think that, in respect to historical truths only, it was consistent with the dignity of Supreme Wisdom to instruct mankind in a human manner; that is, by means of words and writings; and to let miracles and extraordinary things take place in nature, when they were required as evidence of authority and credibility. But the eternal truths, so far as they are of use for the welfare and happiness of man, on the contrary, God teaches in a manner more to suit the Godhead; not by words or written characters, which may be intelligible, here and there, to this or to that man; but by creation itself, and its internal relations, which are legible and intelligible every where, and to all men. Nor does he certify them by signs and miracles, which effect only historical belief; but he stirs the mind created by him, and affords it an opportunity to observe those relations of things, to observe its own self, and to become persuaded of the truths of which it is destined to acquire a knowledge here on earth.

I, therefore, do not believe, that the resources of human reason are inadequate to the persuading of mankind of the eternal truths requisite for their happiness; and that God had need to reveal them to them in a preternatural manner. They who maintain this, deny the omnipotence or the goodness of God in another way, that, which, in one way, they imagine they are attributing to his goodness. He was, in their opinion, good enough to reveal to mankind the truths on which their happiness depends; but he was neither omnipotent nor good enough to grant to them the faculties of discovering them themselves. Besides, by this assertion, they make the necessity of a supernatural revelation, more universal than revelation itself. For if without revelation, the human race cannot but be depraved and miserable, why have by far the greater portion thereof, been living without true revelation from the beginning, or why must both the Indies wait until the Europeans are pleased to send them some comforters, to bring them tidings, without which they can, in the latter's opinion, live neither virtuously nor happily, tidings, which, in their situation, and with their fund of intelligence, they can neither rightly comprehend, nor properly avail themselves of?

According to the notions of true Judaism, all the inhabitants of the earth are called to happiness; and the means thereof are as extensive as the human race itself; as liberally dispensed as the means of preventing hunger and other natural wants. Here, man is left to rude nature, which internally feels its powers and uses them, without being able to express himself in words and discourse, otherwise than defectively, and, as it were, stammering; there aided, by science and art, and brightly shining in words, figures and similes, whereby the perceptions of the inward sense are transformed into, and exhibited in a distinct system of symbols.

Whenever it was of use, Providence caused wise men to rise up amongst all nations, and bestowed on them the gift of clear-sightedness around and within themselves, in the works of God, and that of imparting their knowledge to others. But that is neither required, nor of any great utility at all times. Very frequently, as the Psalmist says, "The lisping of babes and sucklings is sufficient to shame the enemy." Man living in simplicity, has not yet artfully contrived the exceptions so puzzling to a sophist. With him the word "Nature," or the mere sound of it, has not become a being that wants to supersede the Godhead; he even knows yet little of the difference between direct and indirect agency; but he hears and sees the all-vivifying power of God everywhere, in every rising sun, in every fall of rain, in every blowing flower, and in every lamb that pastures on the meadow, and cherishes life. There is something not altogether correct in this representation; nevertheless it directly leads to the knowledge of an invisible and almighty being, whom we have to thank for all the blessings we enjoy. But when an Epicurus, a Helvetius, or a Hume criticise the defects of that representation, and — which is excusable in human nature — extravagate on the opposite side, and want to carry on a juggling game with the word "Nature;" Providence again raises up amongst the people, men, who separate prejudice from truth, who correct extremes on either side, and show that truth will endure although prejudice be rejected. In the main, the material is still the same; here, with all the native and vigorous sap with which nature provided it; there with the refined savor of art; of lighter digestion, it is true; but for valetudinarians only. The doings and forbearings of mankind and the morality of their conduct, may, perhaps, expect as good a result of that crude and plain representation, as of those refined and purer ideas.

Many a people is destined by Providence to wander through that circle of ideas, nay, sometimes, to go round it more than once; but, perhaps, at those multifarious epochs, the quantity and measure of its morality will have been upon the whole about the same. I, for my own part, have no conception of a "training of the whole human race," such as ray late friend Lessing himself let some historiographer of mankind put into his head. They imagine to themselves, the thing "human race," as a single individual, and think. Providence has put it here on earth, as it were, in a school, to be trained from an infant to an adult. In the main, the human race (if the metaphor will hold good) is, in almost every age, infant, adult, and greybeard at once, only in different places and regions. Here, in the cradle, sucking the breast, and living on cream and milk; there, in manly armor and eating the flesh of oxen; and again in another place, tottering on a staff, and toothless once more. Progress is for individual man, who is destined by Providence to pass a portion of his eternity here on earth. Every one goes his own way through life. One's route leads him over flowers and meadows; another's across desert plains, over steep mountains or by the side of dangerous precipices. Yet they all get on on the journey, pursuing the road to happiness, to which they are destined. But that the bulk, or the whole human race here on earth, should be constantly moving forward in progress of time, and perfectioning itself, seems to me not to have been the design of Providence. It is, at least, not so decided, nor by far so necessary for the vindication of Providence, as some are wont to think.

That we should forever spurn theories and hypotheses, talk of facts, want to hear of nothing but facts, and yet look least for facts, where facts are most wanted! Do you want to divine the design of Providence with man? Then forge no hypotheses; look only around you at what actually does pass — and if you can take a general view of the history of all ages — at what has passed from the beginning. That is fact; that must have belonged to the design; that must have been approved of in the plan of Wisdom, or at least have been admitted in it. Providence never misses its aim. That which actually happens, must have been its design from the beginning, or have belonged to it. Now, in respect to the human race at large, you do not perceive a constant progress of improvement, that looks as if approaching nearer and nearer to perfection. On the contrary, we see the human race, as a whole, subject to slight side swings; and it never yet made some steps forward, but what it did, soon after, slide back again into its previous station, with double the celerity. Most nations of the earth pass many ages in the same degree of civilization, in the same crepusculous light, which appears much too dim to our spoiled eyes. Now and then, a particle of the grand mass will kindle, become a bright star, and run through an orbit, which, now after a longer, now after a shorter period, brings it back again to its stand still, or sets it down at no great distance from it. Man goes on; but mankind is constantly swinging to and fro, within fixed boundaries; but, considered as a whole, retains, at all periods of time, about the same degree of morality, the same quantity of religion and irreligion, of virtue and vice, of happiness and misery; the same result, when the same is taken into account against the same; of all the good and evil as much as was required for the transit of individual man, in order that they might be trained here on earth, and approach as near to perfection as was allotted and appointed to every one of them.

I now come home again to ray previous observation. Judaism boasts of no *exclusive* revelation of immutable truths indispensable to salvation; of no revealed religion in the sense in which that term is usually taken. Revealed *religion* is one thing, revealed *legislation* is another. The voice which was heard on *Sinai*, on that memorable day, did not say, " I am the Lord, thy God, the eternal, self-existing Being, omnipotent and omniscient, who rewards men, in a future life, according to their works." All this is the *universal religion of mankind*, and not Judaism. And it was not the universal religion of mankind, without which they can be neither virtuous nor saved, that was to be revealed there. In the main, it could not; for whom were the voice of thunder, and the sound of trumpets to convince of those eternal tenets of salvation? Surely, not the animal man, to whom his own reflections had never yet suggested the existence of an invisible Being, that rules and governs this visible world; him the marvellous voice would not have inspired with ideas, and, therefore, could not have convinced. Still less would it have convinced the sophist, about whose ears so many doubts and cavils are buzzing that he is no longer able to discriminate the voice of sound common sense. *Logical demonstration* is what he demands; no miracles. And if, for the sake of confirming an *immutable truth*, the founder of a religion raise up from the earth all the dead that ever walked on it, still a sceptic would say: the teacher has raised many dead, it is true, but about the immutable truth I am no wiser than before. Now I know that some one is able to do, and to cause to be heard, extraordinary things; but there may be several such beings, who may not think proper to reveal themselves just now: besides, how very short does all this fall of the infinitely sublime idea of an *only eternal* Godhead, who rules this universe after his own unlimited will, and sees into the most secret thoughts of men, to reward their works, according to their merits, if not always here, still hereafter! He, who knew nothing about this, who was not penetrated with the truths so indispensable to human happiness, and thus unprepared went up to the holy Mount, him the stupendous and wonderful array might stun and awe, but not teach him better. No; all that was supposed to be already known, or, perhaps, was taught and explained by human reasoning, and placed beyond all doubt, during the days of preparation. And now the divine voice called out, "*I am the Lord thy God, who led thee out of the land of Egypt; who delivered thee from bondage, &c.*" An historical fact, on which the legislation of that *particular people* was to be founded, since laws were to be revealed there; commandments, judgments, but no immutable theological truths. "I am the Lord, thy God, who made a covenant with thy forefathers, Abraham, Isaac, and Jacob, and swore to them to form out of their seed a nation of my own. The time has, at last, arrived, when that promise is to be fulfilled. For that purpose I delivered you from the bondage of the Egyptians. I delivered you thence, amidst unheard-of miracles and signs. I am your deliverer, your chief, and king; I make a covenant even with you, and give you laws, after which ye shall live, and become a happy nation, in the land which I shall put ye in possession of." All these are historical truths, from their nature, resting on historical evidence, which *must* be attested by authority, and *may* be corroborated by miracles.

According to Judaism, miracles and extraordinary signs are no evidence either for or against *immutable self-evident truths*. Hence Scripture itself directs, that if a prophet teach or counsel things which are contrary to decided truths, we are not to hearken to him, even if he confirm his legation by miracles; nay, if he seek to entice to idolatry, we are to put the wonder-doer to death. For miracles can only attest depositions, support authorities, and confirm the credibility of witnesses; but all depositions and authorities together cannot subvert a decidedly self-evident truth, nor yet place a questionable one above doubt and suspicion.

Now, although that divine book, which we have received through Moses, is supposed to be properly a code of Law, and to contain judgments, rules of life, and precepts; yet it is well known to include withal an inscrutable treasure of self-evident truths and theological dogmas, which are so identified with the laws as to form but one whole with them. All the laws are referable to or are founded on immutable self-evident truths, or put one in mind of, and cause one to ponder on them: hence our Rabbins justly observe, that the laws and dogmas stand in the same relation to each other as the body does to the soul. I shall have occasion to say more about this further on, and here content myself with presupposing it as a fact, of which every one may convince himself who looks for that purpose into even any translation of the books of Moses. Many ages of experience also teach that this divine code of law has become a source of information to mankind, at which they draw new ideas, or amend the old. The more you search therein, the more you are amazed at the depth of knowledge hid in it. At a first view, truth, indeed, presents itself in it, in the plainest garb imaginable, and almost without any pretensions whatsoever. But the nearer you approach, the chaster, the more innocent, affectionate, and wishful the look with which you are gazing at her, the more she will unfold to you of her divine beauty, over which she throws a thin gauze, that it may not be profaned by vulgar and unholy eyes. All those excellent theorems are, nevertheless, presented to knowledge and proposed for meditation, without being forced upon belief. There is not, amongst all the precepts and tenets of the

Mosaic law, a single one which says, "Thou shalt believe this," or "Thou shalt not believe it;" but they all say, "Thou shalt do," or "Thou shalt forbear." There, faith is not commanded; for that takes no commands, but what get to it by the road of conviction. All the commandments of the Mosaic law are addressed to the will of man, and to his acting faculty. Nay, the word in the original language, which they are wont to translate "to believe," in most cases, properly means "to trust in," "to rely on," "to have full confidence in what is promised or caused to be expected." "Abraham trusted the Lord, and it was counted to him for piety." (Gen. xv. 6.) "The Israelites saw, and had confidence in the Lord, and in his servant, Moses." (Exod. xiv. 31.) Wherever the question is of eternal self-evident truth, there is nothing said of believing, but *understanding* and *knowing*. "Know, therefore, this day, and consider it in thine heart, that the Lord he is God, in heaven above, and upon the earth beneath; there is none else." (Deut. iv. 39.) "Hear, O Israel, the Lord our God is a unity." (Deut. iv. 4.) In no place is it said, "Believe, O Israel, and thou shalt be blessed; forbear doubting, O Israel, or this or that punishment shall betide thee." Commandments and prohibitions, rewards and punishments, are for actions only, for life and morals, all which depend on man's will and pleasure; and are governed by notions of good and evil, and, therefore, also by hope and fear. Belief and doubt, assent and dissent, on the contrary, are not to be regulated by our volition; not by wishes and desires; not by fear and hope, but by our discernment of truth or untruth.

For this reason, too, ancient Judaism has no symbolical books, no *articles of faith*. No one needed be sworn to symbols; to subscribe to articles of faith. Nay, we have not as much as a conception of what is called *oaths of creed*; and, according to the spirit of true Judaism, must hold them inadmissible. It was Maimonides who first conceived the thought of limiting the religion of his forefathers to a certain number of principles: "in order," says he, "that religion, like all sciences, may have its fundamental ideas, from which all the rest is deduced." In this merely casual thought originated the thirteen articles of the Jewish Catechism, to which we are indebted for the beautiful morning-hymn, *Yigdal*, and some good writings by Chisdai, Albo, and Abarbanel. And these are all the consequences they have been attended with hitherto. Into religious fetters, thank God! they have never yet been forged. Chisdai disputes them, and 'proposes alterations; while Albo diminishes them, and will allow no more than three, which tolerably well agree with those suggested by Lord Herbert of Cherbury, for the catechism, in later times; and still others, particularly Lorja and his disciples, the modern Cabalists, will not admit at all of any fixed number of fundamental tenets, but say, "In our doctrine everything is fundamental." However, that dispute was carried on, as all such disputes should, with earnestness and zeal, but without rancor or asperity; and notwithstanding Maimonides's thirteen articles were adopted by the majority of the nation, no one, as far as I know, has ever declared Albo a heretic, for his attempt to limit them, and lead them back to far more general axioms. In this matter, we have not disregarded the important judgment of our sages, viz. "Although one loosens, and the other binds, they are both teaching the word of the living God."[20]

In the main, here, every thing depends even on the difference between *believing* and *knowing*; between theological *dogmas* and religious *commandments*. All human knowledge may certainly be limited to a few fundamental ideas, which are laid down as a basis. The fewer there are, the more solid the building will be. But laws admit of no abridgement. In them every thing is fundamental; and so far we may, on good grounds, say, to us all the words of Scripture, all God's commandments and prohibitions are fundamental. If, nevertheless, you wish to have the quintessence of them, mark how that eminent teacher of the nation, Hillel the elder, who lived before the destruction of the second temple, took himself in the matter. "Rabbi," said a Pagan to him, "wilt thou teach me the whole law while I am standing on one leg?" Samai, to whom he had made the same proposal before, dismissed him with contempt; but Hillel, celebrated for his imperturbable temper, and his mildness, said, " Son, love thy neighbour like thyself. This is the text of the law; all the rest is commentary. Now go thy ways, and study."

I have now sketched the outlines of the ground plan of ancient original Judaism, such as I conceive it to be: systems and laws, persuasions and actions. The former were not bound to words or written symbols, which were to continue always the same, for all men, for all ages, all periods, amidst all the changes of language, manners, modes and relations of life, which were always to offer us the same inflexible forms, into which we cannot force our ideas without mutilating them. They were intrusted to living, intellectual instruction, which may keep pace with all the changes of times and circumstances, and be altered according to a pupil's exigencies, and suited to his abilities and powers of comprehension. It was both the written book of the law, and the ceremonial duties which a follower of Judaism had constantly to discharge, that occasioned that paternal mode of teaching. In the beginning, it was expressly forbidden to write more on the law than God had caused Moses to signify to the nation. " What has been delivered to thee orally," say the Rabbins, " thou art not permitted to put down in writing." And though writing on the law had become absolutely necessary, in the sequel, it was with extreme reluctance that the heads of the synagogue determined on consenting to it. They called that licence, the destruction of the law; and said with the Psalmist, "There is a time when we must make a law void for the sake of the Lord." (Ps. cxix. 126.) But according to the original polity, it was not to be so. The ceremonial law itself is a kind of living writing, which rouses the mind and the heart: it is full of meaning; it never ceases to excite meditation, and constantly gives inducement and opportunity for oral instruction. What the pupils themselves did, from morning till night, and what they saw others do, was a direction to religious dogmas and persuasions it impelled them to follow their teacher's footsteps, to watch them, mark all their actions, and gather the information of which their talents rendered them capable, and their conduct made them deserving. The diffusion of writings and books which have been multiplied to infinity, in our days, through the invention of the printing press, has entirely transformed man. The great revolution thereby wrought in the whole system of human knowledge and persuasions has, indeed, in one respect, (for which we cannot be too thankful, to beneficent Providence) been of a profitable result to the refinement of our race. Still, like every other acquisition which man may make here below, it has, withal, been productive of many evils, which must be attributed partly to its abuse, partly to the necessary conditions of human nature. We teach and instruct one another by writings only; we learn to know nature and man out of writings only; we toil and repose over, edify and amuse ourselves with writings only. The minister does not entertain his congregation; he only reads or declaims to them a written treatise. The professor rehearses, from the chair, his written quire. Dead letter all; spirit of living conversation none. We are affectionate in letters, and chide in letters; we quarrel in letters, and make it up in letters. Our whole intercourse is epistolary; and when we come together, we know of no other entertainment than a game, or reading to one another!

Hence it came, that man has almost lost his value with his fellowman. Conversation with a sage is no longer sought after; for we find his wisdom in books. All we do is, we encourage him to write, when, perhaps, we fancy he has not consigned enough to the press already. Hoary age has lost its venerableness; for beardless youth knows more out of books than the former from experience. Whether the youth understands it rightly or not, does not matter; he knows it, and that is enough; he has it at his tongue's end, and will put it off with greater assurance than the honest greybeard, who, perhaps, has a readier command of ideas than of words. We can no longer conceive that the prophet should think it so shocking an evil, " that the child shall behave himself proudly against the ancient" (Isaiah iii. 5); or that a certain Grecian should predict the downfall of the state, because some petulant young men were making a laughing-stock of an old man at a public assembly. We do not want the man of knowledge and experience; we only want his writings. In a word, we are proper men of letters.[21] Our entire existence depends on letters: and we scarcely can imagine that a mortal can cultivate or perfection himself without the help of a book.

It was not so in the hoary ages of yore. If it cannot just be said that it was better, it certainly was different. They drew at other sources; they gathered and preserved in other vessels: and what they had thus preserved they distributed singly by quite other means. Man was then more necessary to man; doctrine was more intimately connected with the conduct of life, and so was observance with practice. The uninformed had to closely follow the informed; the disciple, his teacher, to seek his conversation, watch, and, as it were, sound him, in order to gratify his thirst of knowledge. That I may the more plainly show what influence that circumstance had on religion and morality, I must once more be allowed to digress from my road, into which, however, I shall soon turn again. My subject-matter borders on so many others, that I cannot always march on without now and then getting into a by-path.

Methinks, the changes that have taken place in writing characters, at sundry periods of civilization, have had, from the beginning, a very considerable share in the revolutions of human knowledge in general, and in the various modifications of men's ideas and opinions about religious matters, in particular: and if they did not produce those revolutions all itself, they, at least, in a great measure co-operated in them with collateral circumstances. Man scarcely ceases being satisfied with the first impressions of the external senses (and what man can let it rest there long?) he scarcely feels the spur entering his intellect, to form to himself ideas out of those impressions, but he sees the necessity of tacking those ideas to visible characters; not only for the sake of communicating them to others, but also to keep fast hold of them himself, and he able to mind them again as often as may be required. The first step in separating general characteristics, he will make shift, nay, be obliged, to do without characters; for all new abstract ideas must still be formed without characters, and then only have names given them. The common characteristic is, in the first place, by force of attention, to be brought out on the tissue with which it is interwoven, in order to make it conspicuous. What is of great assistance in this is, on the one part, the objective force of the impression, which that characteristic has the power of making upon us; and, on our own part, the subjective interest we take in it. But this bringing out and minding the common characteristic costs the intellect some exertion. The light which attention concentrated on that point of the object soon vanishes again, and becomes lost in the shadow of the mass of which it forms a part. When that exertion requires to be continued for some time, or too frequently repeated, the intellect is unable to get on much further; it has begun to separate, but it cannot think. What help is there for it? Wise Providence has placed within its immediate reach means of which it may avail itself at any time; namely, it tacks, either by a natural or arbitrary association of ideas, the abstracted characteristic to a visible character, which, as often as its own impression is renewed, instantaneously reproduces that characteristic, pure and unmixed, and throws light upon it. In this manner, we know, originated all human languages, composed of natural and arbitrary characters; without which languages man would have but little whereby to distinguish him from an irrational animal; since he can remove scarcely a step from sense without the help of characters.

In the same manner, as the first steps to intellectual knowledge must have been taken, the sciences are enlarged and enriched with inventions even now; and thus, at times, the invention of a new word is of the utmost importance to them. He who first invented the word "Nature," does not seem to have made a particularly great discovery: still it was him, whom his contemporaries had to thank for being able to shame the juggler, who exhibited to them an appearance in the air, and tell him that there was nothing supernatural in his trick, but that it was only an effect of nature. Suppose they had yet no clear conception of the properties of refracted rays, and of the manner in which, by means of them, a figure may be produced in the air (and how far does our own knowledge of them extend, even at this time? Scarcely one step further. For we are as yet but little acquainted with the nature of light, and its component parts), they knew, at least, how to refer a single appearance to a general law of nature, and were not under the necessity of attributing every contrivance to a specific spontaneous cause. So it was also with the discovery that air possesses gravity. Although we are not able to account for gravity itself, we know, at least, to reduce to the general law of gravity, the observation that fluids will rise in air-void tubes, in which at a first view, they should be supposed rather to sink. We may render it conceivable how a rising was effected, in this case, by the general sinking, which we cannot explain; and even that is another step in knowledge. Accordingly, not every word in the sciences is to be, at once, pronounced an empty sound, because it is not derivable from elementary ideas. If it denote the properties of things, to their true extent, it is all that is wanted. There would have been no fault to find with the term "*fuga vacui*," had it not been more general than the observation itself. It was found, that there are instances where nature is in no such great haste to replenish the void; the expression was, therefore, not to be rejected as empty, but as incorrect. Thus the terms cohesion of bodies," and "general gravitation," still continue to be of great importance in the sciences; although we do not yet know how to derive them from fundamental ideas.

Previous to Baron Von Haller's discovery of the law of Brownianism,[22] how many an observer must not have perceived the phenomenon itself in the organic nature of living creatures. But it vanished again at the very first moment, and did not distinguish itself enough from collateral appearances to arrest the observer's attention. Whenever the observation re-occurred, it seemed to him a single effect of nature, which could not remind him of the number of cases in which he had noticed the same thing before. It, therefore, got lost again soon, like the former, and made no lasting impression on his memory. Haller alone succeeded in raising that circumstance out of its connexion, by perceiving its generality, and marking it with a word; since which it has excited our attention, and we know how to refer to a general law of nature every single case in which we notice something analogous.

Thus the marking of ideas is doubly necessary: it is necessary for ourselves, as it were, as a receptacle, in which to preserve them, and keep them near at hand for use; and, next, to enable us to communicate our thoughts to others. Now, in the latter consideration, sounds or audible signs are the more preferable; for when we want to communicate our thoughts to others, the ideas are already present in the mind, and we may, as occasion requires, bring forth the sounds by which they are denoted, and thus become distinctly apprehensible to our fellow-creatures. But in consideration of ourselves they are not so. If we wish to be able to resuscitate abstract ideas in the mind, and bring them to our recollection at any future time by means of signs, the signs must be forthcoming of themselves, and not wait until they are summoned by our will and pleasure, inasmuch as this our will and pleasure presupposes the ideas, which we want to recall to our memory. This is an advantage we derive from visible signs, because they are permanent, and do not require to be brought forth anew on every occasion, in order to make an impression.

The first visible signs which men made use of to stamp their abstract ideas withal, probably were the things themselves; namely, as every thing in nature has a character of its own, whereby it distinguishes itself from all others, so the sensible impression which that thing makes on us, draws our attention, principally, to that distinctive character, awakes the idea of it, and therefore, very conveniently serves to denote it. Thus, the lion may have become a sign of prowess, the dog of fidelity, the peacock of proud beauty; and thus the first physicians carried about them live serpents, to denote that they possessed the art of rendering the noxious harmless.

In course of time, it may have been found more handy to take the figures of the things, either in solid substances or on surfaces, instead of the things themselves; next, and for conciseness' sake, to make use of the outlines; then to let only a part of the outlines stand for the whole, and finally, to compose of several heterogeneous parts, a grotesque whole, still *full of meaning*; and that method of denoting, is what we call *hieroglyphics*.

All this, we see, may have developed itself naturally enough. But the passage from hieroglyphics to our alphabetical characters, that passage seems a leap, and the leap seems to have required more than ordinary human powers.

There is positively no ground for asserting, as some do, that our alphabet consists only of signs of sounds, and that it can no otherwise be applied to things or ideas, but by means of sounds. Writing certainly will remind us, who have a more lively conception of audible signs, of distinct words first: our road from writing to things, therefore, lies in, and through speech; but not necessarily so. To one born deaf, writing is the immediate notation of things; and if ever he recover his hearing, the alphabetical characters will, in the first days, most certainly bring first to his mind, the things immediately connected with them; and then only by means of those very things, the sounds which answer them. The difficulty of passing to our writing, I imagine to consist properly in this; that without any preliminary or inducement, they must have come to the well-considered determination of representing by a small number of elementary signs, and by every possible transposition of them, a multitude of ideas, which, at first sight, would seem, neither to admit of being brought under one view, nor of being arranged in classes, the better to compass them.

There too, however, the process of the understanding has not been altogether without guidance. As they had very oft occasion to change writing for speech, and speech for writing, they might very soon observe that in colloquial language, the self-same sounds frequently return, as do the self-same parts, in some of the hieroglyphic figures; though always in different combinations, whereby their meanings are multiplied. At last, they will have become aware, that the sounds which man is able to put forth and render distinct, are not so infinite in number, as the things which are denoted by them; and that the system of distinct sounds easily admits of being encompassed, and divided in classes. Accordingly, some imperfect experiments of such division, might be made in the beginning, improved and perfected in course of time, and a hieroglyphic character that answered it appropriated to each class. And even then, it will always remain one of the most glorious discoveries made by the human intellect. But, at least, one sees how men could be led, without any flight of invention, but step by step, on the idea of measuring immensity; of, as it were, comparting the starry firmament in figures, and assigning to each single star its station, without even knowing their exact number. Of the audible signs, I think it must have been easier to discover the trace, which they had only to follow, to perceive the figures into which the immense host of human ideas admit of being formed; and then it was no longer so difficult to apply them to writing, to arrange that, too, and divide it into classes. Hence, I suppose, that a people deaf-born, would comparatively have more to exert their inventive powers, in passing from hieroglyphics to alphabetical writing; because in written characters it is not quite so easily seen, that they have an imaginable compass, and admit of being divided into classes. When speaking of the elements of audible languages, I make use of the word "classes;" for in our living and cultivated languages, written characters are not as yet by far so multifarious as speech, and the same letter is differently read and pronounced, in different combinations and positions. Yet it is evident that we have made our colloquial language all the more monotonous, by the frequent use of writing; and, according to the directions and exigencies of writing, also the more elementary. Hence the languages of nations, who know nothing of writing are by far more copious and fertile; and many sounds in them so indeterminate, that we are not able to denote them by our own characters, otherwise than very imperfectly. They must, therefore, have been obliged in the beginning, to take things concretely, and to denote a great many similar sounds, by one and the same written character. But nicer distinctions may have been observed in course of time, and more characters adopted to denote them by. However, that our alphabet has been borrowed of some kind of hieroglyphic writing, we may see even now, by most of the features and names of the Hebrew letters;[23] and in them, as is evident from history, originated all other characters known to us. It was a Phoenician, who taught the Greeks the art of writing.

All those various modifications of writing, and modes of notation, must also have acted differently on the progress and improvement of ideas, opinions, and all descriptions of knowledge; and in one respect, they must have acted in their favor. In astronomy, husbandry, ethics, and divinity, observations, experiments, and speculations were multiplied, propagated, facilitated, and preserved for posterity. These are the cells in which bees collect the honey, and save it for themselves, and for the use of others. But, as it always is with human matters, what Wisdom erects in one place, Folly already pulls down, in another, and, in most cases, avails itself of the very same engines. What was to conduce to the improvement of man's condition, misapprehension on the one hand, and abuse on the other, converted into corruption, and deterioration. What had been simplicity and ignorance, now became seduction and gross error. The multitude were not at all, or only half-instructed in the ideas to be united to those visible signs; they did not look upon the signs as mere signs; but took them for the things themselves. As long as they were making use of the things themselves, of their effigies or emblems instead of the signs, that error was very possible; for besides their signification, the things had their own reality. The coin was, at the same time, substance; and itself of use and service. The ignorant might therefore be the easier mistaken in — and wrongly appreciate — its value as coin. Hieroglyphic writing would, indeed, partly correct that error, or, at least, was not so favourable to it as the outlines: for these were made up of heterogeneous and incongruous parts, uncouth and preposterous figures, which have no existence of their own in nature, and, one would suppose, could not be taken for writing. But the very mysteriousness and oddness in their composition furnished superstition matter for many a fiction and fable.

Hypocrisy and willful abuse were busy supplying the multitude with tales, which the latter had not themselves sufficient ingenuity to invent. He who had once acquired power and consequence, was anxious, if not to increase — at least to conserve it. He who had once given a satisfactory answer to a question, did not like to be at fault, ever after. There is no absurdity so gross, no farce so outrageous, to which they will not resort; no fable so frivolous which they will not put off upon simplicity, merely to be ready with a "therefore" for every "wherefore?" The phrase, "I do not know," becomes inexpressibly bitter, when one has once set up for a man of extensive, perhaps of general, knowledge; especially when station, and office, and dignity, seem to demand we should know. O how must many a one's heart beat, when he is on the point of either losing consequence and consideration, or becoming a traitor to truth; and how few there are who possess the prudence of Socrates, in always replying, at once, "I know nothing," even in things where they are rather more at home than their neighbours, in order that they may save themselves embarrassment, and render humiliation the lighter beforehand, if, finally, such an avowal should become unavoidable.

Meanwhile we see how Zoolatry and Iconolatry, how the adoration of idols, and of human beings, how tales and fables could originate in all this. And if I do not give it out as precisely the fountain-head of heathen mythology, still I believe that it has very much contributed to the birth and dissemination of those absurdities. This will, particularly, serve to explain a remark made by Professor Meiners, somewhere in his works. He thinks he has invariably noticed, that amongst primitive nations, (namely, such as wrought their own improvement without being indebted to others for their civilization), Zoolatry has been more in vogue than Antholatry; nay, that inanimate things were adored and worshipped, in preference to human beings. Supposing the remark to be correct, and leaving the philosophical historian to vouch for the same, I shall try to illustrate it.

Whenever mankind adopt things themselves, their figures or outlines, as signs of ideas, they can select none more convenient or significant to denote moral properties withal than animals. And that, for the reasons which my friend Lessing, in his Treatise on Fables, assigns to Aesop, for making animals the acting personages in his Apologue. Every animal has a definite distinctive character, and shows itself from that side, at first view, as its entire conformation mostly points to this its peculiarity. One animal is agile; another is sharp-sighted; one fierce; another gentle; one faithful, and attached to man; another treacherous and fond of liberty, and so forth. Even inanimate things have something more defined in their exterior than man has: he, at first view, bespeaks nothing, or rather every thing; he possesses all those properties, at least, he is quite destitute of none of them, nor does the more or less show itself at once on the surface. His distinguishing characteristic, therefore, is not conspicuous; and of all things in nature, he is least fit for denoting moral ideas or properties withal.

In the Plastic arts, even now, gods or heroes cannot be identified better than by the animals or inanimate things conjoined with them. Although a Juno may differ from a Minerva, even in the figure, still they are much easier distinguished by their characteristic animal-accompaniments. Poets, too, when they want to speak of moral qualities in metaphors or allegories, mostly have recourse to the brute creation. The lion, tiger, eagle, bull, fox, dog, bear, worm, dove, are all expressive, and their meaning obvious. Thus, they might, in the beginning, seek to indicate by such emblems, and embody in a visible shape also the attributes of any being that, of all others, appeared to them most worthy of adoration; and in the necessity under which they were of tacking those most abstract of all ideas to visible things, and to such visible things, too, as admitted of fewest significations, they must have been obliged to fix upon animals, or compose certain figures out of several of them. And it has been seen how so innocent a thing, a mere mode of writing, will very soon degenerate in the hands of man, and pass into idolatry. Naturally, therefore, all original idolatry will be found to have consisted of the worship of animals more than of human beings. The latter could not be made use of at all for denoting divine attributes; and their frequent deification must have come from another quarter. Heroes, conquerors, or sages, legislators or prophets, perhaps, arrived amongst them from happier climes, and so distinguished themselves, and appeared illustrious by their extraordinary talents, that they were adored as messengers of the Deity, if not as the Deity itself. It will, however, be conceived that such is more likely to be the case with nations who are not indebted to themselves for civilization, but to others; since — as the common adage says — a prophet is seldom much esteemed in his own country. And thus Mr. Meiners' remark would be a kind of confirmation of my hypothesis, that the want of writing characters has been the first occasion of idolatry.

This is also the reason that, in judging of the religious notions of a people unknown to us in other respects, we ought to take care not to view every thing with our own home-bred eyes, lest we should call idolatry what, in the main, is nothing but writing. Figure to yourself another *Otaheitan*, neither knowing any thing about the secret of the art of writing, nor having been gradually inured to our ideas, were all at once transplanted from his own part of the world to one of the most unpictorial temples in Europe; and to render the instance the more striking, say, to the temple of Providence. He finds it bare of images and decorations, save, on the further white stuccoed wall, some black lines and dots, which chance might trace there.[24] O no; the whole congregation are looking at those lines and dots with reverential awe, and with their hands folded address their petitions to them. Now let him be as suddenly and rapidly conveyed back to *Otaheite*, and there give his inquisitive countrymen an account of the theological notions in vogue at the D. . . . *Philanthropin*.[25] Would they not both laugh at, and lament the gross superstition of their fellow-creatures, who had sunk so low as to pay divine adoration to a parcel of black lines and dots on a white wall? Similar mistakes our own travellers may have frequently committed, when describing to us the religions of remote nations. A foreigner must make himself very intimately acquainted with the thoughts and opinions of a people before he can undertake to say that, with them, images still retain the spirit of writing, or that they have already degenerated into idolatry. At the sacking of the Temple of Jerusalem, the invaders found the cherubim in the ark of the covenant, and took them for the idols of the Jews. They saw every thing with barbarian eyes, and in their own point of view. Conformably to their manners, they took an emblem of Divine Providence, and Sovereign Mercy, for a representation of the Godhead, or for the Godhead itself, and chuckled over their supposed discovery. Thus, even now, readers cannot help smiling at the Indian philosophers, who suppose this universe to be born by elephants, which elephants they place on a huge tortoise, which tortoise is held up by an enormous bear, and which bear stands on a prodigiously large serpent. Perhaps the question never occurred to the good folks; and what does the prodigiously large serpent stand upon?

Now read, in the *Hindoo Shaster* itself, the passage describing an emblem of this kind, which, probably, has given occasion to that tradition. I extract it from the second volume of *Accounts of Bengal, and the Empire of Hindostan, by J. Z. Hollwel*, who got himself instructed in the sacred books of the *Gentoos*, and was able to see with the eyes of a native Bramin. These are the words in the eighth section: —

"*Modu* and *Kytu* [two monsters, *Discord* and *Rebellion*] had been vanquished; and now the Lord emerged from invisibility, and glory environed him on all sides."

"The Lord said: thou *Brama* [creative power] create and form all things of the new creation, with the spirit which I breathe unto thee. And thou, *Vishnu* [preservative power] protect and preserve the created things and forms, according as I direct thee. And thou, *Sieb* [Destruction — Transformation], transform the things of the new creation, and remodel them, with the power I shall give thee."

"*Brama*, *Vishnu*, and *Sieb*, heard the words of the Lord, bowed, and showed obedience."

"Thereupon Brama floated on the surface of *Johala* [Ocean], and the children of *Modu* and *Kytu* fled and disappeared, as he presented himself."

"When the spirit of *Brama* had caused the commotion of the abysses to subside, *Vishnu* transformed himself to a mighty bear [with the Gentoos an emblem of strength, because it is the strongest of all animals, in proportion to its size], descended into the abysses of *Johala*, and with his tusks, drew forth to light *Murto* (the earth), whereupon there spontaneously sprang out of it a mighty large tortoise [with the Gentoos, an emblem of stability], and a mighty large serpent [their emblem of wisdom], and *Vishnu* erected the earth on the back of the tortoise, and put *Murto* on the head of the serpent, &c."

All this is found amongst them also depicted in figures; and one sees how easily such emblems and hieroglyphics may lead to errors

The history of mankind, it is well known, has run through a period of many ages, during which real idolatry had become the prevailing religion, almost over the whole face of the earth. Figures had lost their value as signs. The spirit of truth, which was to be preserved in them, had evaporated, and the insipid vehicles, which remained behind, turned to destructive poison. The notions of the Godhead, which still maintained themselves in the popular religions, were so deformed by superstition, so corrupted by hypocrisy and priestcraft, that it might be questioned, on good grounds, whether Atheism be not less detrimental to human happiness, or ungodliness not less ungodly, than such a religion? Human beings, brute animals, trees, nay, the most hideous, the vilest things in nature, were adored and worshipped as deities, or rather feared as such. For of the Godhead, the national public religions of those days had no other notion than that of a terrible being, superior in power to the inhabitants of the earth, soon put in anger, but difficult to propitiate. To the reproach of both the human understanding and the human heart, superstition would contrive to combine ideas the most incompatible, and admit human sacrifices, and worshipping of animals, at one and the same time. In the most magnificent temples, constructed and embellished according to all the rules of art (shame on reason! — as Plutarch exclaims) — you looked in vain for the divinity adored there, but found an altar raised before a frightful baboon; and to that obscene animal blooming youth and virgins were immolated. So deeply idolatry had debased human nature! And as the prophet expresses it, in that emphatical antithesis, "They slaughter human beings, to offer them as sacrifices to brutes!"

Philosophers occasionally tried to check the general depravity, to refine and enlighten ideas, either publicly or by secret institutions. They sought to restore to the figures their former significations, or even superadd new ones to them, and, as it were, thereby again breathe a soul into the dead body. But all in vain: their rational interpretations had no effect on the religion of the common people. Eager as uncultivated man seems to be after explanation, as dissatisfied he feels when it is given him in its real simplicity: he soon gets weary of, and spurns what is intelligible to him, and constantly goes in quest of new, mysterious, and inexplicable things, which he catches up with redoubled pleasure. His inquisitiveness must be always upon the stretch, and never gratified. Public speaking, therefore, met with no hearers amongst the majority of the nation; and, on the contrary, with the most obstinate opposition on the part of superstition and hypocrisy; and received its usual reward, con- tempt, or hatred, or persecution. The secret institutions and provisions, for the purpose of maintaining, in some measure, the rights of truth, partly themselves took the road of corruption, and became nurseries of all kinds of superstition, of every species of vice, of every description of infamy. A certain school of philosophers conceived the bold thought of keeping human ideas quite apart from every thing figurative, or like it; and tacking them to such Meriting signs, as, from their nature, cannot possibly be taken for any thing else, namely, to *Numbers*. As numbers represent nothing in themselves; and as there is no natural connexion between them and any impression on the senses, one would suppose they do not admit of being misunderstood; they must either be taken for arbitrary writing signs, or be given up as unintelligible. There, one should think, the rudest understanding cannot confound signs with things; and that by that ingenious expedient every abuse was obviated. To him, who docs not understand numbers, they are unmeaning figures. Him, whom they do not enlighten, at least they do not seduce.

So might the founder of that school imagine. But ignorance soon took again to its old courses. Not satisfied with what was found so intelligible and conceivable, they sought after an occult virtue in the numbers themselves; again, for an inexplicable reality in the signs, whereby their use as signs were again lost. They believed, o rat least made others believe, that in those numbers were hidden all the secrets of nature, and of the Godhead; ascribed to them miraculous powers, and pretended to satisfy with, and by means of them, not only mankind's curiosity and thirst of knowledge, but even the full extent of their vanity; their aspiring at sublime and unattainable things; their inquisitiveness and egotism; their avarice and frenzy. In one word, imbecility had again defeated the plan of wisdom, and again destroyed, and even applied to its own rule, what the latter had provided for a better purpose.

And now I am able to set forth with greater distinctness my conjectures about the purpose of the ceremonial law in Judaism. The first parents of our nation, Abraham, Isaac, and Jacob, continued true to the Lord, and sought to preserve amongst their families and descendants ideas of religion, pure and far distant from all idolatry. These, their descendants, were, in the sequel, selected by Providence to be a *nation of priests*; that is, a nation, which, by its regular institutions and polity, its laws and practices, its fortunes and changes, should constantly point to sound and unvitiated notions of God and his attributes; and never cease to teach, proclaim, preach, and conserve them amongst all other nations, as it were, merely by its own existence. They sojourned amongst barbarians and idolators, under extreme oppression; while misery almost made them as insensible of truth as arrogance had made their oppressors. God released them from this state of bondage by extraordinary deeds of wonder; he became the deliverer, leader, lawgiver, and law administrator of the nation thus formed by himself; and so ordered the whole of its polity as to make it answer the wise designs of his providence. But man's eyes are weak and shortsighted. Who can say: 'I penetrated into God's Sanctuary; I have looked into the whole of his plan, and can accurately state the magnitude, extent, and bounds of his designs?' A modest inquirer, however, may be allowed to conjecture, and draw conclusions from his conjectures, if he but always bear in mind that he can do nothing but *conjecture*.

It has been seen, what difficulty there is in preserving the abstract ideas of religion amongst mankind, by permanent signs. Figures and hieroglyphics will lead to superstition and idolatry; and our own alphabetical writing makes man too speculative. It exhibits the symbolical meaning of things, and of their mutual relations, by far too openly on the surface; it saves us the labour of diving and searching, and forms too wide a separation between doctrine and life. In order to remedy those defects, the lawgiver of that nation gave *the ceremonial law*. Religious and moral information was to be united with the ordinary and daily transactions of men. The law, indeed, did not urge them to meditation; it only prescribed to them acts; only what they had to do and to forbear. It seems to have been a grand maxim with that polity, that to act, man must be urged; but to meditate he can only be induced. Accordingly, every one of those actions, every custom, every ceremony thus prescribed, had its meaning, and cogent reason, — was closely allied to the speculative study of theology and ethics, and a stimulus to the searcher after truth, to meditate on those sacred things himself, or ask one more experienced than himself for information. For it was the principal object and fundamental rule of that polity, that the truths useful to the welfare of the nation at large, as well as to each individual, should be as distant from every thing figurative as possible. They were to be bound up with practices and observances, which were to serve them for signs, without which they could not be preserved.

The acts of man are transient; in them there is nothing stable, nothing continuate, which, like hieroglyphics, may, through abuse, lead to idolatry. But then, they have that advantage over alphabetical signs, that they do not isolate man, and make of him a recluse, continually brooding over writings and books; on the contrary, they urge him to social commerce, to copying, and to living oral instruction. Hence, there were but few written laws; nor were even these quite intelligible without oral instruction and tradition; and it was forbidden to write more on them. Whereas the unwritten laws, the living instruction of man to man, from the mouth to the heart, were to explain, enlarge, restrict, and more particularly determine, what, for wise purposes and with wise moderation, was left undetermined in the written law. In every thing a youth saw doing, in all public as well as private functions, on all gates and doorposts, whichever way he turned his eyes or ears, he met with something which excited him to think and search; which induced him closely to follow the footsteps of one older and wiser than himself; observe with filial diligence, and copy with filial docility, even his most trivial actions and observances; enquire after their meaning and object, and gather what information his teacher might think suitable to his abilities and fitness. In this manner, were doctrine and conduct, prudence and industry, speculation and conversation, most intimately united, or, at least, should have been, according to the lawgiver's original disposing and design. But the ways of God are inscrutable; and within a short period, this too took the road of corruption. It was not long before that bright orbit too was run round; and things again returned to no great distance from the depth from which they had emerged, as, alas! is manifest since many ages.

Already, in the first days of this so marvellous a legislation, the people relapsed into the sinful delusion of the Egyptians, and demanded a *Zoological image*. And from what they pretended, it seems that they did not demand it exactly as a Deity, for the sake of adorning it; for with that, the high-priest, the legislator's own brother, would not have complied, if his life had been ever so much in danger. They merely spoke of a divine Being, which should lead them on, and supply the room of Moses, who was supposed to have deserted his post. Aaron could no longer withstand the people's importunities; he cast them a calf; and that he might keep them firm in their intention not to offer up divine adoration to that image, but to God alone, he called out, "Let tomorrow be a feast to the Lord." On the feast-day, however, while regaling themselves, and dancing, the rabble let him hear quite different language. "These," shouted they, "be thy gods, O Israel, which have brought thee up out of the land of Egypt." Now the fundamental law was broken through; the national bond was dissolved. Sensible reasoning is seldom of much use with an excited mob, when disorder has once got the upper hand; and we know to what hard measures the lawgiver had to make up his mind, for the sake of quelling the rebellion of the mixed multitudes, and to bring them back to subordination. It deserves, nevertheless, to be noticed and admired, how divine Providence knew to turn that unfortunate circumstance to advantage, and for what sublime ends, altogether worthy of itself, it employed it.

It has been remarked, in a former place, that paganism had even more tolerable notions of the *power* of the Godhead than of its *goodness*. A common man takes goodness and easy reconcilableness for weakness; he envies every one the least pre-eminence in power, wealth, beauty, honor, &c., but not pre-eminence in goodness. Indeed, how should he; since it mostly depends on himself to arrive at that degree of gentleness which he thinks enviable? It requires some thinking to comprehend that rancor and vindictiveness, envy and cruelty, are, in the main, nothing but weakness, nothing but the effect of fear. Fear, combined with chance and precarious predominance, is the parent of all those barbarous feelings. Fear only renders man severe and implacable. He who is fully conscious of his superiority, feels far greater happiness in leniency and forgiveness.

When we have once learned to see this, we can no longer feel any hesitation in considering mercy, at least, as sublime a quality as power; in thinking the Supreme Being, to whom we attribute omnipotence, capable also of love; and in acknowledging in the God of power also the God of mercy. But how far was paganism from being thus refined? You do not find in the whole of its mythology, in the poems, and other remains of the ancient world, a trace of their having attributed to any one of their deities also love and clemency towards the children of men. "The people, as well as the majority of the most renowned captains and enlightened statesmen, indeed, took the gods whom they adored, for beings mightier than man; but for such as had, in common with them, the same wants, passions, foibles, and even the same vices. So malicious did the gods, in general, appear to the Athenians, and other Grecians, that they fancied any extraordinary or long-lasting success to draw on it the anger and grudge of the gods, and to be overthrown by their instrumentality. They further imagined those same gods so irascible, that all unfortunate accidents were looked upon as divine judgments; not for a general depravity of manners, or of great individual crimes, but for slight, and, mostly, inadvertent omissions, in certain rites and solemnities.[26] In Homer himself, in his gentle and benign soul, the thought had not yet kindled, that the gods forgive out of love; and that without beneficence, they would know no bliss in their empyreal abode.

Now mark with what wisdom the lawgiver of the Israelites makes use of their horrible offence against majesty, to promulgate to mankind so very important a doctrine, and to open to it a source of consolation, from which we are drawing and refreshing ourselves, even to this day. What sublime and awful preparation! The mutiny had been subdued; the sinners were brought to a sense of their guilty attempt; the nation plunged into the deepest sorrow, and Moses, the Lord's nuncio himself, almost desponding. "O Lord" said he, "as long as thy displeasure has not subsided, carry us not up from hence. For wherein shall it be known that I and thy people have found grace in thy sight? so shall we be separated, I and thy people, from all the people that are on the face of the earth."

"I will do this thing also that thou hast spoken;" was the Lord's reply, *'for thou hast found grace in my sight, and I have known thee by name."

"Upraised by those solacing words," resumed Moses, "I presume to make another, and a still bolder request. O Lord, I beseech thee shew me thy glory."

I will make all *my goodness* pass before thee,[27] and make thee acquainted with the name of the Lord, in what manner I am gracious to him, to whom I am gracious, and show mercy to him to whom I show mercy. Thou shalt look at the back part of my presence, for my face cannot be seen."[28] Thereupon the vision passed by before Moses, and a voice was heard saying, "The Lord is, was, and shall be eternal, being, all-mighty, all-merciful and all -gracious; long-suffering and abundant in goodness and truth, who preserves his goodness even to the thousandth generation; who forgives transgression, sin and apostasy; but lets nothing pass by unresented." What man's feelings are so hardened, that he can read this with dry eyes? Whose heart is so inhuman that he can still hate his fellowman and remain irreconcilable to him?

The Lord, indeed, says: that he will let nothing pass by unresented; and those words are known to have been the occasion of much error and misconstruction. But if they are not completely to set aside that which precedes them, they immediately lead to the grand thought, which our Rabbins discovered in it, namely, *to let man pass by nothing unresented, is also an attribute of divine love and mercy.*

Once, in conversation with a highly esteemed friend of mine, about theological matters, he asked me, "Did I not wish to obtain, by direct revelation, the assurance that I shall not be miserable in a future state V He was of one opinion with me, that I need not be in fear of eternal punishment in hell; since God cannot let one of his creatures be unceasingly miserable; nor can any creature, by his actions, have deserved the punishment of being miserable for ever. The hypothesis that the punishment of sin must be proportionate to the offended majesty of God, and, therefore, infinite, my friend, with several other eminent men of his church, had discarded long ago, which therefore precluded all debate between us on that subject. The idea of duties to God, which is correct only by half, has occasioned the just as undeterminate idea of *offences against the majesty of God*, while the latter idea, taken in a literal sense, brought into the world the inadmissible notion of eternal punishment in hell, the farther abuse of which made not fewer people *really* miserable in this world, than, *theoretically*, it makes unhappy in the next. My philosophical friend also agreed with me, that God created men for their happiness; and that he gave them laws for their happiness. Then, if the slightest infraction of those laws be punished in proportion to the lawgiver's majesty, and therefore carry with it eternal misery, God has given men those laws for their destruction. Were it not for the laws of so infinitely exalted a being, man would not be liable to eternal misery. Why, if mankind might be less miserable without divine laws, who doubts that God would have spared them the fire of those laws, since it must so irretrievably consume them? All that being admitted, my friend put his query in a more definite form: "Must I not wish to be assured by a revelation, that I shall be exempt even from terminable misery in a future state?"

"I must not," replied I; "that misery can be nothing more than well-deserved punishment; and, in God's paternal household, I am willing to undergo the chastisement which I deserve."

"But what, if all-merciful God would remit men even justly deserved punishment?"

"That he certainly will, as soon as punishment shall be no longer indispensable to men's amendment. There is no need for a direct revelation to convince me of that. When I infringe the laws of God, the moral evil makes me unhappy; and divine justice, that is, his *all-wise love*, seeks to lead me to moral recovery, by means of physical misery. When that physical misery, that punishment of sin, is no longer absolutely necessary to a change of my principles, I am, without a revelation, as persuaded as I am of my own existence, that my father will instantly remit the punishment; and, on the contrary, if that punishment be still of service for my moral recovery, I do not, by any means, wish to be acquitted of it. In the state of that paternal regent, a transgressor suffers no other punishment but that which he himself must be desirous of suffering, if he could see its effect and consequences in their true light."

"But may not God think fit to let man suffer as an example to others; and is not an exemption from such exemplary punishment desirable?

"No," replied I; "in God's dominions no individual suffers merely for the good of others. If that were done, such immolation for the good of others must impart to the sufferer himself a higher moral worth; and, in consideration of the internal accession of perfection, it must be of importance to himself to have promoted so much good by his suffering. Since, then, it is thus, I cannot *dread* such a state; I cannot *wish* for a revelation that I shall never get into a condition of magnanimous benevolence, so fortunate both to my fellow-creatures and myself. What I have to dread is the sin itself. When I have committed a sin, Divine Punishment is an act of benevolence towards me, an effect of his paternal mercifulness. When it ceases to be a benefit to me, I am certain it will instantly be remitted. Can I wish that my father would turn away from me his chastising hand, before it has effected what it was designed to effect? When I am praying that God may let a transgression of mine pass by entirely without punishment, do I know what I am praying for? O, of a surety, it is also one of the attributes of infinite Divine Love, that he lets not any transgression of man pass by entirely without punishment. Surely

"Omnipotetice belongeth to the Lord alone:
Unto thee, God, belongeth also mercy,
When to every one thou renderest according to his works."

Ps. lxii. 12, 13.

That the doctrine of God's mercifulness was first promulgated to the nation by Moses, on that grand occasion, the Psalmist expressly declares in another place, when he quotes, from the former's books, the identical words in question here: —

"He made known his ways unto Moses, his acts unto the children of Israel.

"The Lord is merciful and gracious, slow to anger, and plenteous in mercy.

"He will not always chide, neither will he keep his anger for ever.

"He hath not dealt with us after our sins, or rewarded us according to our iniquities.

"For as the heaven is high above the earth, so great is his mercy toward them that fear him.

"As far as the east is from the west, so far hath he removed our transgressions from us."

"Like as a father pitieth his children, so the Lord pitieth him that fear him.

"For he knoweth our frame; he remembereth that we are dust." &c. (Ps. ciii.)[29]

Now I am able to concentrate my ideas of Judaism of former times, and bring them under one focus. Judaism consisted, or, according to the founder's design, was to consist of

1. Religious dogmas and propositions of immutable truths of God, of his government and providence, without which man can neither be enlightened nor happy. These were not forced on the belief of the people, by threats of eternal or temporal punishment, but suitably to the nature and evidence of immutable truths, recommended for rational consideration. They needed not be suggested by direct revelation, or promulgated by words or writing, which are understood only m this or that place, at this or that time. The Supreme Being revealed them to all rational beings, by events and by ideas, and inscribed them in their soul, in a character legible and intelligible at all times, and in all places. Hence sings the frequently quoted bard:

"The heavens tell the glory of God; and the firmament showeth his handy work.

"One day streams this unto another, and night therein instructeth night."

"No lesson or words of which the voice is not heard; their chord rings through the entire globe; their discourse penetrates to the extremes of the inhabited world, where he set a tabernacle to the sun, &c." (Ps. lxx. 1.)[30]

Their effect is as universal as the salutary influence of the sun, which, while revolving round its orbit, diffuses light and heat over the whole globe, as the same bard still more distinctly declares, in another place:

"From where the sun rises to where it sets, the name of the Lord is praised." Or, as the prophet Malachi says, in the name of the Lord: "From where the sun rises to where it sets, my name is great among the Gentiles; and in all places, incense, sacrifice, and pure meat-offerings are offered unto my name, for my name is great among the heathen."

2. Historical truths, or accounts of the occurrences of the primitive world, especially memoirs of the lives of the first ancestors of the nation; of their knowledge of the true God, even of their failings, and the paternal correction immediately following thereon; of the covenant which God entered into with them, and his frequent promise to make of their descendants a nation dedicated to himself. These historical truths contain the groundwork of the national union; and, as historical truths, they cannot, according to their nature, be received otherwise than *on trust;* authority alone gives them the necessary evidence. And they were, moreover, confirmed to the nation by miracles, and supported by an authority which sufficed to place *faith* beyond all doubt and hesitation.

3. Laws, judgments, commandments, rules of life, which were to be peculiar to that nation; and by observing which, it was to arrive at national — as well

as every single member thereof, at individual happiness. The lawgiver was God himself; God, — not in his relations as Creator and Preserver of the universe — but God, as Lord Protector and ally of their forefathers; as the liberator, founder, and leader, as the king and ruler of that people. And he gave the laws a sanction, than which nothing could be more solemn; he gave them publicly, and in a marvellous manner never before heard of, whereby they were imposed on the nation, and on their descendants for ever, as an unalterable duty and obligation.

Those laws were *revealed*, that is, they were made known by the Lord, by *words*, and *in writing*. Still, only the most essential part thereof was entrusted to letters; and without the unwritten laws, without explanations, limitations, and more particular definitions, even those written laws are mostly unintelligible, or must become so in course of time; since neither any words or written characters whatever retain their meaning unaltered, for the natural age of man.

As *directions to general practice*, and rules of conduct, both the written and the unwritten laws have public and private happiness for their immediate object. But they must also be mostly considered as a mode of writing; and as *ceremonial laws*, there is sense and meaning in them. They lead inquiring reason to divine truths; partly to eternal, partly to historical truths, on which the religion of *that* nation was founded. The ceremonial law was the bond for uniting practice with speculation, conduct with doctrine. The ceremonial law was to offer inducements to personal intercourse and social connexion between the school and the professor, the inquirer and the instructor, and to excite and encourage competition and emulation; and that purpose it actually did answer in the first times, before the polity degenerated, and human folly again intermeddled to change, by ignorance and misguidance, good to evil, and the beneficial to the hurtful.

Under that primitive polity, state and religion were not *united*, but *one*; not *allied*, but *identical*. The relations of man to society, and the relations of man to God, converged into one point, and could never come in collision. God, the Creator and Preserver of the universe, was, at the same time, the king and administrator of that nation; and he is a *Unit*, which admits of no division or plurality, either politically or metaphysically. Nor has that regent any wants, and he demands nothing of the nation but what is for their good, or what promotes the happiness of the state; the same, as on the other hand, the state could demand nothing that was contrary to the duties to God; but rather what was prescribed by God, that nation's lawgiver, and the administrator of their laws. Hence, civil life amongst that nation assumed a holy and religious cast, and every service to the public was, at the same time, *true divine service*. The congregation was a congregation of the Lord; their concerns were the Lord's; the public taxes were heave- offerings to the Lord; and, to the least measures and regulations for the public safety, every thing was religious. The Levites, who lived on the public revenue, received their maintenance of the Lord. They were to have no part or inheritance in the land; *for the Lord is their inheritance.* He who is obliged to roam about abroad *worships foreign gods.* In several passages in Scripture, this cannot be taken in a literal sense, and, in the main, means nothing else but *that he is subjected to foreign laws; laws which are not, at the same time, religious, like those of his own country.*

And now as to offences. Every offence against the authority of God, the lawgiver of the nation, was an offence against majesty, and, therefore, a political or state offence. He who reviled God, committed high treason; he who wickedly broke the Sabbath, abrogated, as far as lay with him, a fundamental law of civil society; for on the institution of that day rested a material part of the polity. "The Sabbath shall be an eternal covenant between me and the children of Israel, says the Lord, a perpetual sign, that in six days," &c. (Exod. xxxi.) Therefore, under that polity, those offences could, nay must, be punished civilly, not as false opinions, not as *misbelief,* but as *misdeeds,* as contumacious political offences, which aim at the abolishing, or at least at weakening, the lawgiver's authority, and, thereby, undermining the state itself. And yet, with what lenity were not even those highly treasonable offences punished! What plenteous allowance was there not made for human frailty! According to a certain traditional law, sentence of death could not be passed on a delinquent, *unless he have been cautioned by two unexceptionable witnesses, who must have cited to him the exact law, and threatened him with the penalty thereby enacted.* Nay, where corporeal or capital punishments were concerned, *the delinquent must have admitted, in express words, the punishment, taken it upon himself, and forthwith committed the offence in the sight of the witnesses.* Under such regulations, how rare must capital executions have been; and what frequent opportunities judges must have had of sparing themselves the painful necessity of passing sentence of death on their fellow-creatures, their fellow-images of God! *A hanged man is a disrespect to God,"* says Scripture. How long must judges have paused, how long must they have examined and considered mitigating circumstances, before they signed a sentence of death! Nay, more. According to the Rabbins, every criminal court, which cares about a good name, ought to mind that, during a period of *seventy* years, no more than one person suffer punishment of death.

This clearly shows how little one must be acquainted with the Mosaic code and the Jewish polity, to believe that it authorises ecclesiastical law, and ecclesiastical power; and attaches temporal punishment to unbelief or misbelief. Both *the Searcher after Light and Right*, and *Mr. Moerschel* are, therefore, very far from being right in thinking that I have set aside Judaism, by my arguments against ecclesiastical law and ecclesiastical authority. Truth cannot contradict truth. What divine law commands, reason, not less divine, cannot set aside.

It was not unbelief, not false doctrine or error, that was punished; but contumacious offences against the majesty of the lawgiver, daring misdeeds against the fundamental laws of the state, and the civil government; and it was punished only then, when the crime, in licentiousness, exceeded all bounds, and was approaching to rebellion; when the offender did not mind having the law quoted to him by two fellow-citizens, and being threatened by them with the regular punishment; nay, not even taking the punishment upon himself, and committing the offence in their sight. This is tantamount to high treason, and the religious reprobate becomes a state criminal. Besides, the talmudical doctors expressly declare, *that ever since the destruction of the temple of Jerusalem, all corporeal and capital punishment, nay, all fines, so far as they were merely national, ceased to be legal.* Now this perfectly accords with my principles, and cannot be explained except on them. The civil bonds of the nation were dissolved; religious infractions no longer constituted state offences; and religion, as such, knows of no punishment, of no penitence, but what a repentant sinner voluntarily imposes upon himself. It disclaims all coercion, acts with the wand "gentleness" only; and acts only on the mind and the heart. Let them try to explain rationally the above talmudical assertion any other way than on my principles.

Methinks I hear many a reader ask: "Wherefore all this prolixity to tell us so notorious a thing? Judaism was a hierocracy, an ecclesiastical government, a state of priests, or, if you please, a theocracy. It is well known what assumptions such a government will indulge itself in."

By no means. All those technical terms throw on the subject a false light, which I had to avoid. We want to be always classifying and dividing all things in categories. So that we know under what category a thing must be brought, we are satisfied, let our conception of it be ever so imperfect in other respects. But wherefore seek a generic term for a thing which belongs to no genus at all, which ranks with nothing, which cannot be brought under any category whatever? That polity did exist once, and once only: call it by its individual name, the *Mosaic* polity. It has disappeared; and omniscient God alone knows among what people, and in what age something like it will again appear.

Plato supposes a terrestrial Cupid as well as a celestial. Just so one may say, there are terrestrial politics as well as celestial. Take one of those gay adventurers with whom the promenades of every great city abounds — one of those lady-killers, — and enter with him into conversation about *Solomons Song*, or about the Loves of our first Parents in Paradise, as described by *Milton*. He will think you are ranting, or want him to hear you say your task how to beset the heart of a prude with Platonic blandishments. Just as little will a fashionable statesman understand you, when you are extolling to him the simplicity and moral excellence of that primitive polity. Just as the former knows of love nothing but sensual gratification, so the latter, when treating of politics, will talk of nothing but an imposing attitude, circulation of money, commerce, balance of power, population; and to him religion is a means of which the legislator avails himself to curb restive man, and the priest to suck the blood out of him, and consume his marrow.

This false point of view, in which we are wont to contemplate the true interest of human society. I had to remove out of the reader's sight. I, therefore, did not call the subject by any name, but endeavoured to exhibit it itself to him, with all its properties and purposes. When we look point blank at true politics, we shall discover in them — as a certain philosopher said of the sun — a divinity, where ordinary eyes see only a pebble.

I have said that the Mosaic institution did not subsist long in its pristine purity. Already, in the days of the prophet Samuel, the building got a rent, which widened more and more, until all its parts came asunder. The nation wished to have a visible king for their regent, a king in the flesh. Whether the priesthood had already begun to abuse their consequence amongst the nation, as we are told in Scripture of the high-priest Eli's sons, or whether the people's eyes were dazzled by the splendour of neighbouring royalty; suffice it to say, they demanded *a king, to judge them like all the nations* (1 Sam. viii. 5). Indignant at their proposal, the prophet represented to them what sort of thing a king in the flesh was, who has peculiar wants, which he may multiply at his will and pleasure; and how difficult it is to satisfy a frail mortal, to whom the rights of the

Godhead had been granted. But all in vain; the people persisted in their resolution, their request was complied with, and they experienced every thing the prophet had foretold them. Now the polity was undermined; the unity of interest destroyed. State and religion ceased to be identical; and a collision of duty was already no longer impossible. Still, instances of it must have been rare, while yet the king himself not only was of the nation, but also observed the laws of his native land. And now let us follow history through a long series of fortunes and vicissitudes, through several good and several bad, several virtuous and several profligate reigns, down to the sad times in which the founder of the Christian religion delivered the cautious decision: "Render unto Caesar the things which be Caesar's, and unto God the things which be God's." (Luke XX. 25.) An evident discrepancy: a collision of duty! The state was under foreign dominion, and receiving mandates, as it were, of foreign gods, all the while that the national religion, with its influence on civil rights, still remained in preservation. Here is demand against demand; claim against claim. Whom are we to render to? Whom are we to obey? Then bear both burdens as well as ye may — the decision fell out — serve two masters with patience and acquiescence: render unto Caesar, and render also unto God, to each his due; now that the unity of interest is destroyed.

And a more wholesome advice could not be given to the house of Jacob, even at this very day, Comply with the customs, and the civil constitution of the countries in which ye are transplanted, but, at the same time, be constant to the faith of your forefathers. Bear both burdens as well as ye may. It is true, that, on the one hand, the burden of civil life is made heavier to you on account of the religion to which you continue faithful; while, on the other, the climate under which you live, and the times, render the observance of your religious laws more burdensome than they really are. Hold out, notwithstanding; remain immoveable on the station which Providence assigns to you, whatever may befall you; which is no more than what your prophets foretold you, long ago.

Indeed, I do not see, how those who were born in the house of Jacob can, in any conscientious manner, disencumber themselves of the law. We are allowed to think on the law, to inquire into the spirit of it; and, here and there, where the law-giver assigned no ground, conjecture one, which, *perhaps*, was governed by times, circumstances, and local situation; and, *perhaps*, will undergo modification, according to times, circumstances, and local situation — whenever the Supreme Legislator shall be pleased to make known to us his will thereon; and make it known to us as loudly, publicly, and as utterly beyond doubt and hesitation, as he made known to us the law itself. As long as that does not take place, as long as we cannot produce so authentic a discharge from the law, all our fine reasoning cannot exonerate us from the strict obedience we owe to it; while the awe of God will always draw a line between theory and practice, beyond which no conscientious person will permit himself to go. I, therefore, repeat the protest I first entered. The eye of man is weak and shortsighted. Who can say: "I have got into God's holy of holies; I have seen through the whole system of his purposes; and can fix its measure, aim, and bounds? I am at liberty to suppose, but not to decide; not to act according to my supposition. Why, even in human matters, I dare not presume to act on my own supposition, and explain away laws without the legislator's or judge's leave; how much less, then, in things divine?" Laws necessarily connected with the possession of land, and with local institutions, carry their dispensation with them. Without a temple, and a priesthood, and, out of Judea, neither sacrifices, nor a law of purification, nor contributions to the priests, as far as they depended on landed property, any longer obtain. But personal commandments, duties which were imposed on a son of Israel, without any consideration of the temple service or landed property in Palestine, must, for aught we can see, be observed strictly to the letter of the law, until it shall please the Most High to make our conscience easy, by loudly and openly proclaiming their abrogation.

Then it evidently comes down to this: what God has bound, man cannot dissolve. If one of us even go over to the Christian Church, I cannot conceive how he can believe, thereby, to compound with his conscience, and exonerate himself from the yoke of the law. Jesus of Nazareth never signified that he was come to acquit the house of Jacob of the law; nay, he said the reverse in express terms; and, which is still more, he *acted* the reverse. Jesus of Nazareth himself kept, not only the Mosaic law, but also the Rabbinical institutions; and whatever seems to be contrary to this, in the sayings and proceedings recorded of him, only seems so at first sight. Carefully examined, every thing will be found perfectly to agree, not only with Scripture, but also with tradition. If he came to put a stop to the more and more spreading Pharisaism and hypocrisy, surely he would not himself have set the first example of them, by sanctioning, by his own observance, a law which he thought should be abrogated and set aside. On the contrary, the Rabbinical maxim, that *he, who is not born in the law, need not bind himself to the law; but he, who is born in the law, must live according to the law, and die according to it*, obviously characterises his whole conduct, and that of his disciples, in the beginning. If, on later times, his followers thought differently, and believed they might absolve also the Jews, who joined them, it certainly was not done by his authority.

And ye, good brethren and fellow-men, who follow the doctrine of Jesus, should you blame us for practising what the founder of your religion himself practised? Should you think you may not love us in return as brethren, not unite with us as citizens, as long as we distinguish ourselves outwardly by the ceremonial law, as long as we do not partake of viands or intermarry with you, all which, for ought we can see, the founder of your religion would neither have done himself, nor have allowed us to do? If that be your real feeling, and is to continue so — which we cannot suppose of Christian-minded men — if civil union cannot be obtained on any other term than that of departing from the law, which we consider still binding upon us, we are heartily sorry for what we deem necessary to declare — that we will rather renounce civil union: then may that philanthropic man, *Dohm*, have written to no purpose, and every thing remain in the bearable state in which it is now, or in any other, your own humanity may think fit to change it. To compromise, is not, here, in our power; but if we be just, it is in our power to love you like brethren, notwithstanding; and in a brother-like manner intreat ye to make our burdens as bearable as ye can. Look upon us, if not as brethren and fellow-citizens, at least, as fellow-creatures and countrymen. Show us the way and supply us with the means of becoming *more efficient* men and countrymen; and let us also enjoy as much of the rights of man as times and circumstances will admit of. We cannot, in conscience, depart from the law; and of what use would it be to you, fellow-citizens void of conscience?

But, in this manner, how can the prophecy be fulfilled, that *a time will come when there will be only one shepherd and one flock?"*

Dear brethren, who mean well with humanity, do not let yourselves be deluded. For to belong to such an ubiquitary shepherd, the entire flock needs neither graze on one field, nor go in and out the master's habitation by one door. This is not what the shepherd wants; nor would it be good for the thriving of the flock. Is it that they are confounding ideas, or designedly seeking to perplex them? They tell you, that a union of religion would be the shortest road to the brotherly love and brotherly toleration, which you, kind-hearted people, so much long for. They will have you imagine, that when we are all of one creed, we shall no longer hate one another on account of religion, or difference of opinion. Then religious animosity will be seized by the root, and extirpated: then the scourge will be wrested out of the hand of hypocrisy, the sword out of the grasp of fanaticism, and the halcyon days will arrive of which it is said: "The wolf shall dwell with the lamb, and the leopard by the side of the goat, &c." The meek souls who propose this are ready to set to work, meet together as negotiators, and humanely take the trouble of bringing about a universal concordat of religions. They will bargain for *truths*, in the same manner as for *rights and privileges*, as for a vendible commodity, ask a price, bid and bate, bully or coax, hurry and cozen one another out of them, until, at length, the parties shake hands, and the treaty for the happiness of the human race wants only to be written down. There are many, indeed, who reject such a project as unfeasible and chimerical; but, nevertheless, talk of a union of religions as of a very desirable state, sincerely pitying the human race on account of that summit of happiness not being reachable by human powers. Friends of mankind, beware listening to such sentiments without putting them to a rigid test. They may be snares, which fanaticism, grown powerless, wants to lay for liberty of conscience. That enemy of all that is good, you know, is of a variety of shapes and forms: the ferocity of the lion, and the mildness of the lamb; the simplicity of the dove, and the cunning of the serpent; no quality is so foreign to it, that it does not either possess it, or knows how to assume it, for the sake of attaining its sanguinary purposes. Now, that through your salutary efforts, it has been deprived of open power, perhaps, it puts on the mask of meekness, to impose upon you; feigns brotherly love, and cants general toleration, all the while that it is secretly forging the fetters in which it means to put human reason, that it may, unawares, hurl it back again into the pool of barbarism, out of which you have begun to extricate it.[31]

Let this not be supposed mere imaginary fear, or the natural effect of an atrabilious temper. In the main, if an union of religions be at all feasible, it can be of none but the worst consequences to reason and to freedom of conscience. For supposing them to be all of one mind about the articles of faith they propose to introduce and establish; supposing them to have accomplished symbols, with which none of the religions prevailing in Europe, at present, has any fault to find; and what would have been effected then? Shall we be all of the same opinion about theological truths? He that has the least knowledge of the construction of the human understanding will believe no such thing. Then the unanimity would lie only in the words, and in the formulae. It is that which the consolidators of religions mean to join for; they want to nip, here and there, a bit off the notions; keep here and there stretching and enlarging the meshes of terms, and make them become so flimsy and indefinite, that the ideas, notwithstanding their inward variety, would scarcely be contained in them. Every one would then, in fact, associate with one and the same word a different idea, peculiar to himself; and ye would boast of having consummated a union of the different creeds of mankind; of having brought the whole flock under one single shepherd! Oh, if there be at all a design in this so specious a pretence, I fear it is that of, in the first place, penning up again the human mind, as yet free. The shy thing will then let itself be caught easily, and suffer the halter to be thrown on its neck. Only tack religion to symbols, opinions to words, to as modest and pliant words as ever you please; only appoint, once for all, the articles; and woe unto the unfortunate, who comes a day after, and criticises even upon those *modest* and pliant words! He is a disturber of the peace. To the stake with him!

Brethren! if it be genuine piety you are aiming at, let us not feign consonance, when manifoldness is, evidently, the design and end of Providence. None of us feels and thinks exactly alike with his fellowman; then wherefore impose upon one another by deceiving words? We are, alas! prone enough to do so, in our ordinary transactions, in our general conversation, comparatively of no material importance; but wherefore also in things involving our spiritual and temporal welfare, and constituting the whole purpose of our creation? God has not stamped on every man a peculiar countenance for nothing: why, then, should we, in the most solemn concerns of life, render ourselves unknown to one another, by disguise? Is not this resisting Providence so far as with us lies? is it not frustrating the designs of creation, if it were possible, and purposely acting against our vocation and destiny, both in this life and that to come? Regents of the earth! if an insignificant fellow-in-habitant of it may be allowed to lift up his voice unto ye, O listen not to the counselors, who, in smooth words, would misguide you to so pernicious an undertaking. They are either blind themselves, and cannot see the enemy of mankind lurking in ambush; or they want to blind you. If you hearken to them, our brightest jewel, freedom of conscience is lost. For your happiness' sake, and for ours, *religious union is not toleration;* it is diametrically opposite to it. For your happiness' sake, and for ours, lend not your powerful authority to the converting into a law any *immutable truth*, without which civil happiness may very well subsist; to the forming into a public ordinance any theological thesis, of no importance to the state: Be strict as to the life and conduct of men; make that amenable to a tribunal of wise laws; and leave thinking and speaking to us, just as it was given us, as an unalienable heirloom; as we were invested with it, as an unalterable right, by our universal father. If, perhaps, the connexion of privilege with opinion be too prescriptive, and the time have not yet arrived to do away with it altogether, at least, endeavour to mitigate, as lies with you, its deleterious influence, and to put wise bounds to prejudices now grown too superannuated;[32] at least, pave, for happier posterity, the way to that height of civilization, to that universal forbearance amongst men, after which reason is still panting in vain. Reward and punish no doctrine; hold out no allurement or bribe for the adoption of theological opinions. Let every one who does not disturb public happiness, who is obedient to the civil government, who acts righteously towards you, and towards his fellow-countrymen, be allowed to speak as he thinks, to pray to God after his own fashion, or after that of his forefathers, and to seek eternal salvation where he thinks he may find it. Suffer no one to be a searcher of hearts, and a judge of opinions in your states; suffer no one to assume a right which the Omniscient has reserved to himself. *"As long as we are rendering unto Caesar the things which are Caesar's; render ye, yourselves, unto God the things which are God's. Love truth! Love peace!*

TRANSLATOR'S NOTES

[1] Talmud tells us that Rabbi Meir, who had himself a great number of scholars, whom he instructed in the Law, nevertheless visited every day his own former teacher, to whom he was indebted for education, accomplishment, and knowledge, in order still to learn from him much of what was good and useful, although the latter had been long known as an apostate who had forsaken the Law. — Rabbi Meir's Pupils, to whom their Professor's tolerant spirit as well as his converse with what they esteemed a depraved person, seemed highly pernicious, expressed to him their surprise at it. "I found a savoury nut," replied he, "of which I keep the kernel, and throw away the shell."

[2] Nor did Providence fall short in its liberality, in this respect, to the Hebrew nation; but bestowed on it meritorious characters who, with love of truth, vanquishing all fear of man, and frequently at no small sacrifice, took care to introduce a more eligible way of thinking amongst their co-religionists, and thus wrought good, as far as their limited sphere would permit.

The names of *Maimonides, Aben Ezra, Manasseh Ben Israel*, &c. &c. are indelibly fixed in the memory of the Hebrew nation; their works are replete with instructive truths and useful information.

I shall have frequent occasion, in the course of this work, both to quote the writings of those great men, and to insert sketches of their lives, and leading characteristics.

[3] I scarcely need refer to the tolerant prayer offered up by King Solomon at the Dedication of the Temple.

[4] Bellarmin himself narrowly escaped being declared a heretic by Pope Sixtus V, for giving him only an indirect dominion over the temporalities of kings and princes. His work was inserted in the catalogue of the Inquisition.

[5]*Anmerkungen zu Abbts freundschaftlichen Correspondenz* 28.

[6] It is objected that, in time of war, a soldier is qualified to kill an enemy, without the latter being in duty bound to suffer it.

But it is not as a man that the soldier is so qualified, but only as a citizen, or as the mercenary of one of the contending powers. A state really is, or pretends to be wronged, and that it can obtain redress no otherwise than by force of arms. The battle is, therefore, properly not between man and man, but between state and state. Of the two belligerents, evidently, one only can have justice on his side. The offender is certainly in duty bound to make reparation to the offended, and to put up with every thing without which, the latter cannot be reinstated in his rights.

7 When individuals of different persuasions form a matrimonial alliance, it is stipulated in the marriage contract, after which of the two principles the domestic establishment shall be conducted, and. the children be trained. But how is it, when, after marriage, one of the parties changes religion, and goes over to another church? In a small work which pretends to have been written at Vienna, and which I shall bave occasion to quote more largely in the following section. (*Das Forschen nach Licht und Recht*. A Search after Light and Right). Such a case is said to be now pending in that capital. A newly-converted-Jew expressly demands to continue living with his wife, who herself abides by the Mosaic faith; and a law-suit has been commenced in consequence. The author of the above-named pamphlet decides according to the liberal system; "It may be reasonably expected," says he "that difference of religion will not be considered a sufficient reason for a divorce. The wise Emperor Joseph will not allow a change of theological dogmas to undo social ties."

Very prematurely judged, I should think! The Emperor no less just than wise, I trust, will hear also the arguments on the other side, and not suffer the liberal system to be abused of for oppression and tyranny. If marriage be only a civil contract, (as, even on Roman Catholic principles, it can be nothing else, between a Jew and Jewess) the words and conditions of the contract must be construed and interpreted, conformably to the meaning of the contracting parties, and not according to that of either the legislator or the judge. If from the principles of the contracting parties, it can be affirmed with certainty that they understand certain words in this, and no other way; and if they had been asked, would have explained them in this, and in no other way, that morally certain affirmation must be admitted as a tacit and implied condition of the contract, and stand just as good in a court, as if it had been explicitly agreed upon. Now it is evident that on signing the contract, the married couple, then both still professing the Mosaic religion, at least externally, meant nothing else but to conduct their joint household after Jewish precepts, and bring up their children to Jewish principles. At all events, the party with whom religion was a consideration, could have supposed nothing else; and if at that time a change of that sort had been apprehended, and the clause proposed, she would have declared herself in no other way. She was aware of nothing else, she expected nothing else, but that she should commence a household after her own parent's rules of living, and procreate children to be trained after her own parent's principles. If the difference be of consequence to that party, if it be notorious that the difference of religion must have been of consequence to her, at the time of closing the contract, the contract must be interpreted according to her notions and persuasions. Suppose the country at large should entertain a different opinion on the subject, it would have no effect on the interpretation of the contract. The husband changes principles, and embraces another religion. If the wife be compelled to enter upon a mode of housekeeping repugnant to her conscience; to bring up children on principles not her own; in a word, if she be compelled to accept, and to have forced upon her conditions of the marriage contract, to which she never agreed, she is evidently wrongfully dealt with; they evidently suffer themselves to be beguiled by insinuations of liberty of conscience, into the most senseless tyranny of conscience. The conditions of the contract can now no longer be fulfilled. The husband, who has changed principles is, if not in *dolo*, at least *in culpa*, that they can no longer be fulfilled. Is the wife to suffer violence of conscience, because the husband demands freedom of conscience? Did she ever consent to it? Could she consent to it? Is not conscience free on her part too? Must not the party who occasioned the change, answer for the consequences of it, make compensation to the other, and reinstate her in her previous situation, so far as that can possibly be done? Can there be any thing more simple? The thing, I should think, speaks for itself. No one can be compelled to accept conditions of a contract, to which, from his principles, he could not have agreed.

With respect to the education of their joint children, both parties have an equal right; If we had such things as neutral training establishments, children, in such contested cases, should be neutrally trained in one of them, until they arrive at the age of reason, and are able to make a choice themselves. But so long as no such institutions are provided, so long as our training establishments stand in connexion with positive religion, a preference is evidently due to the party who remained true to the previous principles, and made no change in them. This, too, very naturally follows from the above principles; and when the contrary takes place anywhere, it is tyranny, and religious oppression. An Emperor no less just than wise, surely will not tolerate in his dominions, so outrageous an abuse of ecclesiastical power.

[8] To this very intelligible definition of ideas, I was lead by that philosophic jurist, my worthy friend, Counselor *Klein*, with whom I had the pleasure of conversing on the subject. His theory of covenants appears to me both simple and fertile. *Ferguson*, in his "Institutes of Moral Philosophy," thinks he has found the obligation of keeping promises, in the expectation we raise in our fellow-creatures, as well

as in the immorality of deceiving. But from this, it would seem, there results only a conscientious duty. That which I was before in conscience bound to give up of my means, for the good of ray fellow-creatures in general, I am, in consequence of the expectation raised in that particular individual, now, in conscience bound, to part with to him. But what has changed that conscientious duty into a compulsory? This, methinks, indispensably requires the principles of resigning, in general, and those of deciding cases of collision, in particular, as they are demonstrated above.

[9] The words "service, honor, &c." have quite a different meaning when referring to God, than when referring to man. Divine worship is not a service which I am rendering God. Honoring God is not an honor which I am conferring upon him. For the sake of preserving the terms, they altered their import. The common man, however, still sticks to the meaning he has been used to, and is firmly attached to his idiom; whence much confusion has arisen in theological matters.

[10] Sacrifice and offering thou didst not desire; mine ears hast thou opened. Psal. xl. 6.

[11] Deut. iv. 5.

[12] In a state, in other respects tolerably liberal, a certain college composed of learned and distinguished men, lately made some dissenters pay double the

regular passing fees. The excuse it offered on being called to account before the authorities was, that dissenters were everywhere "Deterioris conditionis" in civil life. What is most singular is, that double fees continue to be exacted to this very day.

[13] Namely, a clause is valid, and renders a contract binding, when we can conceive a possibility of its having influence on the adjusting of cases of collision. Now, opinions can be brought in connexion with external advantages, no otherwise than by an erring conscience; and it is a question with me, whether they can ever be admitted as a legal stipulation.

[14] In the preface to Manasseh Ben Israel, &c.

[15] Those are the words of ray late friend, Mr. Iselin, in one of his last papers, in the 10th number of the *Ephemeris of Humanity*, Oct. 1782, p. 429. The memory of that true Sage, ought to be perpetual with every one of his contemporaries, who values virtue and truth. It is, therefore, the more inconceivable to me, that I should pass him over, when I was naming the several benevolent persons, who first strove to propagate unlimited toleration in Germany; him, who certainly preached it in our language, and in its widest extent, earlier and louder than any one else. Accordingly I transcribe here, with pleasure, the passage from the advertisement of my Preface to Manasseh Ben Israel, in the Ephemeris, where this is

observed. And this I do, in justice to a man after his death, who himself was so generally just in his life. "The author of the Ephemeris of Humanity fully concurs with Mr. Mendelssohn, also, in what he says about the legislative power of the higher authorities, over the opinions of the citizens; as well as about the agreements which individuals may enter into amongst themselves, concerning such opinions. And this way of thinking, he (the author) has not borrowed only of Messrs. *Dohm* and *Lessing*, but he has been a convert to it already, these thirty years. In the same manner, he also admitted long ago, that what is called religious toleration is not a boon on the part of governments, but a bounden duty." It is impossible to express one's self plainer than in what follows: (*Träume eines Menschenfreundes*, Visions of a Philanthropist, Vol. ii. p. 12.) "Thus if one or more religions are admitted in his dominions, a wise and just sovereign will not think himself entitled to encroach upon their rights, for the benefit of those of his own religion. Every church, every union, whose object is divine worship, is a society to whom protection and justice is due from the sovereign. To deny it, were it even for the sake of favouring the best possible of religions, would be contrary to the spirit of true piety."

"In respect to civil rights, the members of all religious persuasions are perfectly alike; those only excepted, of which the tenets go against the principles of human and civic duties. Such a religion can lay no claim to rights in a state. They who are so unfortunate as to profess it, may expect to be tolerated only as long as they do not disturb the order of society by acts of depravity and injustice. Whenever they do so, let them be punished, not for their opinions, but for their actions." As to the animadversions on the middle-hands in business, which I am said wrongly to impute to Mr. *Iselin*, the circumstances have been quite misrepresented. It was not Mr. *Iselin*, but another, and in other respects a very judicious author, who got an article inserted in the *Ephemeris*, in which he maintains the perniciousness of middle-hands; but who, if anything, was controverted by the editor. The remarks against my co-religionists, made in that article, I shall pass over in silence. This is not the place to appear in their defence. I leave that to Mr. *Dohm*, who can do it with less partiality. Besides, we soon forgive a *Basilean* his prejudices against a people, which he can have no other opportunity of knowing, but from its migratory portion, or from the *Observations d'un Ahacien*. (A very violent pamphlet against the Jews).

[16] There is neither a salary, nor a certain rank in the congregation, attached to the function of circumcising. On the contrary, whoever possesses the requisite habitude, will, with great pleasure, perform

that meritorious work. Nay, the father, on whom properly the duty of circumcising his son is incumbent, has, in most cases, to select one from several competitors, who apply to him for it. All the remuneration, which the operator expects is, the place of honor at the circumcision banquet, and the saying of the benediction after it. According to my theory, which seems so new and hard, all religious offices should be filled in the same manner.

[17] Search for Light and Right. See vol. i. pp. 123, 124; 126, 127; 129: which passages are in the original.

[18] Vol. i. pp. 129, 130.

[19] Vol, i. p. 109.

[20] I have known many a pedant to quote that apothegm, to prove that the talmudical Rabbis pay no regard to the rule of contradiction. I wish I may live to see the day when all the nations of the earth shall admit that exception to the general rule of contradiction: — "The fast of the fourth month, and the fast of the fifth, and the fast of the seventh, and the fast of the tenth, shall be to the house of Judah joy and gladness, and cheerful feasts; only love truth, and peace." (Zech. viii. 19.)

[21] *Buchstaben-menschen.*

[22] *Gesetz der Reitzbarkeit.* Should this term have been wrongly translated, my ignorance of physiology must be my excuse. — Ed.

[23] As א an ox, ב a house, ג a camel, ד a door, ו a hook,

ז a sword, כ the fist or a spoon, ל *stimulus*, נ a fish, ס a support or bottom, צ the eye, פ the mouth, ק an ape, ש the teeth.

[24] The words: *God—Omniscient—Almighty—All-beneficent—Rewarder of Virtue*.

[25] Seminary at Dessau.

[26] *Meiner's Geschichte der Wissenschaften in Griechenland und Rom; zweiter Band*. p. 77

[27] What a sublime import! Thou desirest to behold my whole glory. I will make all my goodness pass before thee. Thou shalt look at the back part of my presence, for my face no mortal man can see!

[28] Exod. xxxiii. 15.

[29] In a general view, the contents of this Psalm are throughout most important. He, to whom the subject is of any interest, will do well to read the Psalm all through with attention, and compare it with the above remarks. It seems to me evidently to have been occasioned by that remarkable passage in Scripture; and to be nothing else but a bursting out of the lively emotion, into which the bard got, on considering that extraordinary event. Accordingly, he commences the Psalm with calling upon his soul to offer up the most solemn thanksgiving to God for the divine promise of his goodness and paternal mercy. "Bless the Lord, O my soul; and forget not all his benefits. He forgiveth all thine iniquities; he healeth all thy diseases; he redeemeth thy life from destruction; he crowneth thee

with loving-kindness and with mercy, &c."

[30] After Mendelssohn's Translation.

[31] Painful experience proves that there is fanaticism even in Atheism. Indeed, but for an admixture of internal Atheism, it never would have become furious. But that even external and open Atheism will become frantic, is as undeniable, as it is difficult to conceive. Although the Atheist, if he be consistent, will always act from *self-interest*; and although it little accords with that, when he sets up for establishing a sect of his own, and does not keep the secret to himself; still he has been known to preach his doctrine with the most glowing enthusiasm, and to become outrageous, nay, prosecute, when his preaching did not meet with a favourable hearing. And a most frightful thing it is, when that kind of zeal inflames a regular Atheist, when innocence gets into the hands of a tyrant, who fears any thing but a God.

[32] We regret to hear also the Congress of the United States (1783) harp on the old string, by talking of an established religion.

Made in the USA
Middletown, DE
02 July 2018